GHOSTS IN THE HUMAN PSYCHE

GHOSTS IN THE HUMAN PSYCHE
The Story of a "Muslim Armenian"

Vamık D. Volkan

PHOENIX
PUBLISHING HOUSE
firing the mind

First published in 2019 by
Phoenix Publishing House Ltd
62 Bucknell Road
Bicester
Oxfordshire OX26 2DS

British Library Cataloguing in Publication Data

A C.I.P. for this book is available from the British Library

ISBN-13: 978-1-912691-06-7

Typeset by Medlar Publishing Solutions Pvt Ltd, India

Printed in the United Kingdom

www.phoenixpublishinghouse.co.uk
www.firingthemind.com

Contents

About the Author

Vamık Volkan, MD, DFLAPA, received his medical education at the School of Medicine, University of Ankara, Turkey. He is an emeritus professor of psychiatry at the University of Virginia, Charlottesville and an emeritus training and supervising analyst at the Washington Psychoanalytic Institute, Washington, DC. In 1987, Dr. Volkan established the Center for the Study of Mind and Human Interaction (CSMHI) at the School of Medicine, University of Virginia. CSMHI applied a growing theoretical and field-proven base of knowledge to issues such as ethnic tension, racism, large-group identity, terrorism, societal trauma, immigration, mourning, transgenerational transmissions, leader–follower relationships, and other aspects of national and international conflict. A year after his 2002 retirement, Dr. Volkan became the Senior Erik Erikson Scholar at the Erikson Institute of the Austen Riggs Center, Stockbridge, Massachusetts and he spent three to six months there each year for ten years. In 2006, he was Fulbright/Sigmund Freud-Privatstiftung Visiting Scholar of Psychoanalysis in Vienna, Austria. Dr. Volkan holds honorary doctorate degrees from Kuopio University (now called the University of Eastern Finland), Finland; from Ankara University, Turkey; and the Eastern European Psychoanalytic Institute, Russia. He was a former president of the Turkish-American Neuropsychiatric Society, the International Society of Political Psychology, the Virginia Psychoanalytic Society, and the American College of

Psychoanalysts. Among many the awards he received are the Nevitt Sanford Award, Elise M. Hayman Award, L. Bryce Boyer Award, Margaret Mahler Literature Prize, Hans H. Strupp Award, the American College of Psycho-analysts' Distinguished Officer Award for 2014, and the Mary S. Sigourney Award for 2015. He received the Sigmund Freud Award given by the city of Vienna, Austria in collaboration with the World Council of Psychotherapy. He also was honored on several occasions by being nominated for the Nobel Peace Prize with letters of support from twenty-seven countries. Dr. Volkan is the author, co-author, editor, or co-editor of more than fifty psycho-analytic and psychopolitical books, including *Enemies on the Couch: A Psychopolitical Journey through War and Peace*. Currently Dr. Volkan is the president emeritus of the International Dialogue Initiative (IDI), which he established in 2007. He continues to lecture nationally and internationally.

About this Book

This book examines the impact of past and present historical events, cultural elements, political movements, and their mental images on the psyche of individuals. Psychoanalysts' attention to such external events while sitting behind their couches and listening to their patients has a long and interesting history. The first two chapters present the history of psychoanalysts' appreciation of the intertwining of external and internal events. Then the story of a successful businessman who called himself a "Muslim Armenian" is told to illustrate how ghosts from the past can remain alive and active in our lives.

The patient featured here is of Hemshin descent. When he started his psychoanalysis in Istanbul, his analyst knew that some individuals from the eastern Black Sea coast of Turkey near the Republic of Georgia and Armenia called themselves *Hemşinli* (the Turkish way of referring to Hemshin people), but she had no knowledge of their Armenian origin. It would be impossible to understand fully some of the important causes of this patient's symptoms and personality characteristics without knowing the history and the culture of the Hemshenis living in Turkey.

I am a psychiatrist and psychoanalyst living in the United States since 1957. As I was born on the Mediterranean island of Cyprus to Turkish parents, my mother tongue is Turkish. I supervised the Turkish psychoanalyst's clinical work while she was treating the businessman whose story is presented in this book. She would call me from Istanbul by phone once a week to discuss the psychoanalytic sessions she had with her patient. She has given her permission to describe her work, but I have changed some of the patient's personal history in order to protect his real identity. These changes will in no way alter the readers' ability to follow this man's psychological journey and recognize how historical ghosts visit communities and enter an individual's inner world.

CHAPTER ONE

History, Culture, Politics, and Psychoanalysis

Sigmund Freud delivered a detailed presentation of his "seduction theory" in April 1896 to the Vienna Society for Psychiatry and Neurology, linking hysterical symptoms to repressed memories of sexual stimulation in childhood. He had come to this conclusion after treating eighteen patients, twelve women and six men, who had a history of sexual molestation by an adult stranger, caregiver, or sibling (Freud, 1896c). His conclusions implied that at the time he was practicing, child sexual abuse was rather common in the Viennese community. By the next year however, in his September 21, 1897 letter to his German Jewish otolaryngologist friend Wilhelm Fliess, Freud expressed skepticism about the stories his patients told. Later, his focus was on new theories on infantile sexuality and the internal worlds of children (Freud, 1905d). He never denied the existence of actual sexual seduction, but he also wrote: "Obviously seduction is not required in order to arouse a child's sexual life; that can also come about spontaneously from internal causes (1905d, pp. 190–191). Focus on the stimuli that come from the child's fantasies for the formation of psychopathology became a key element of the new science called psychoanalysis. In 1933 Freud was still reminding his followers that when he was holding his seduction theory in the 1890s, almost all his women patients told him that they had been seduced by their fathers; but in fact, they were bringing attention to the existence of the female Oedipus fantasy.

Starting in 1925, a major and long-lasting dispute evolved between Freud and the Hungarian psychoanalyst Sándor Ferenczi about the influence of actual trauma—actual sexual abuse—on individuals' internal worlds (Falzeder & Brabant, 2000; Haynal, 2005; P. T. Hoffer, 2010; Paláez, 2009; Rachman, 1997). Clara Mucci (2013) states that "The role of traumatic reality is at the basis … of the conflict between Freud and Ferenczi, and it has to do not only with the clinical practice … but with metapsychology and theory" (p. 46). There is information on how Freud expected total loyalty from his followers (Olsson, in press; Roazen, 1974; Wilson, 1981). In 1932, Freud's followers blocked Ferenczi from delivering a paper that focused on the truthfulness of seduction. This long dispute played a role in the direction taken by other pioneer psychoanalysts, as they continued to follow Freud's path that placed less emphasis during psychoanalytic treatment on the impact of actual seduction coming from the external world and generalized this attitude to include de-emphasis on the impact of other external real events in the appearance of analysands' symptoms and character traits.

Freud and several pioneering analysts were interested in examining history, culture, religion, arts, and other shared external events from a psychoanalytic angle. But, in the clinical setting, the impact of such events on analysands' psyche was not of primary concern. Following World War I, Freud wrote about "war neurosis" and stated that he was not aware

> … that patients suffering from traumatic neurosis are much occupied in their waking lives with memories of their accident. Perhaps they are more concerned with *not* thinking of it. Anyone who accepts it as something self-evident that their dreams should put them back at night into the situation that caused them to fall ill has misunderstood the nature of dreams. (1920g, p. 13)

A few years later he described how war neuroses "opened the eyes of the medical profession to the importance of psychogenesis in neurotic disturbances, and some of our psychological conceptions, such as the 'gain from illness' and the 'flight into illness'" (Freud, 1925d, p. 54). However, the emphasis on the unconscious, to a great extent, screened out the influence of external events and traumas associated with those events, especially when the patient was not an active player in an external event taking place in his or her neighborhood, community, ethnic group, or nation. The focus in the clinical setting was on exploring psychic reality only: an analysand's unconscious conflicts, resistances against exploring them, development of transference neurosis, and their resolution.

In 1932 Freud provided another example that discouraged psychoanalysts from considering such external events, this time major tragedies linked to war and politics. In that year Albert Einstein wrote a letter to Freud asking the following questions: "Is there any way of delivering mankind from the menace of war? … How is it possible for [a small group hungering for political power] to bend the will of the majority, who stand to lose and suffer by a state of war, to the service of their ambitions?" and "Is it possible to control man's mental evolution so as to make him proof against the psychoses of hate and destructiveness?" (Freud 1933b, pp. 199–201). In his response to Einstein, Freud described humans' destructive instinct and stated that "If willingness to engage in war is an effect of the destructive instinct, the most obvious plan will be to bring Eros, its antagonist, into play against it" (p. 212). Thus, he suggested that anything that encourages "the growth of emotional ties" through loving and identification with others operates against war. "This, however, is more easily said than done" (p. 212). He expressed little hope for an end to war and violence or the role of psychoanalysis in changing human behavior beyond the individual level. In 1932, the year I was born, Albert Einstein was fifty-three years old and Sigmund Freud was seventy-six. Anti-Semitism surrounded Freud at that time. A year later Adolf Hitler would be the dictator of Germany. Freud's general pessimism in his response to Einstein was mirrored by many of his followers, although much later Jacob Arlow (1973) would find indications of cautious optimism in some of Freud's writings. I suspect that the Einstein–Freud correspondence has also played a key role in limiting Freud's followers from pursuing the impact of historical, political, and international events on their patients' internal worlds.

John Bowlby (1988) described that when he became an analyst in 1937, psychoanalysts in Great Britain were only interested in the internal worlds of their patients. Paying attention to historical events surrounding patients was considered inappropriate. The followers of Melanie Klein had established themselves as a formidable group in Great Britain competing with ego psychologists. Kleinians—even perhaps more than the ego psychologists—bypassed the influence of traumatizing external historical events while treating their patients. Melanie Klein herself ignored the influences of war while treating one of her patients, a ten-year-old boy named Richard, whose analysis took place while World War II raged, literally overhead, during the

London Blitz under which he and his analyst lived (Klein, 1961). This circumstance was not examined during Richard's analysis. Was ignoring the dangerous external circumstances simply due to Melanie Klein's theoretical stance, or was she avoiding her own emotions related to the external dangers?

Harold Blum's (1985) description of a Jewish patient who came to him for re-analysis in the United States also illustrated a mutual resistance to examining historical events during which both the analyst and the analysand, who belonged to the same large group, were massively traumatized. Blum's patient's first analyst, who was also Jewish, failed to "hear" their large group's shared trauma at the hands of the Nazis in his analysand's material; as a consequence, mutually sanctioned silence and denial pervaded the entire analytic experience, leaving unanalyzed residues of the Holocaust in the analysand's symptoms. Blum wrote:

> Although the patient and his last analyst were both born in Europe and were both Jewish, neither one discussed the experience of debasing bigotry, the war, emigration, being a refugee, social-cultural upheaval, separation from family and friends, and cultural shock. For years, they spoke to each other without mention of each other's accent or why they were meeting in an American rather than a European office. (p. 898)

He continued to state that there was:

> ... a double standard in analysis. Freedom of thought and expression were compromised by tacit cues that some areas were off limits and should remain shrouded in silence. This repetition of the 'conspiracy of silence' (and the suffering in silence of the family) was maintained by depriving memory of emotional meaning, and skillful displacement of discussion. (p. 899)

I can only wonder how many Jewish analysts in the US after World War II were like Blum's patient's former analyst and how many of them, without being aware of it, influenced the application of the psychoanalytic treatment in a way that ignored the Holocaust-related external reality. As Peter Loewenberg (1991) and Leo Rangell (2003) would later remind us, some aspects of a large-group history induce anxiety. I can only imagine that some of these Jewish analysts exaggerated their bias toward a theoretical position called "classical psychoanalysis" that was focused primarily on the patient's conflicts linked to sexual and aggressive fantasies.

In post-World War II Germany as well, there has been both German and German-Jewish analyst-supported resistance to exploring the influence of Nazi era traumas on analysands' psyches and the intertwining of historical external processes with internal conflicts. For example, in the early 1960s, while treating an ethnic German analysand and a Jewish analysand, the well-known German Jewish analyst Anna Maria Jokl left for Israel without completing the two patients' analytic work, and it was not until the mid-1990s that she was able to piece together and report the complex influences that their large-group identities and traumatization by external events had on the scene of analysis. She then focused on mastering their history in the clinical setting (Jokl, 1997).

Before proceeding further, I need to clarify further what kinds of external events were avoided while conducting an individual's analysis. If an analysand's unconscious fantasy was connected with an event in the immediate environment of the analysand's childhood, a "classical" analyst obviously would notice such a connection. Let me give an example, even though it comes from a person who underwent psychoanalysis in recent years. A middle-aged woman had a disagreement with a close female friend and experienced frustration. Soon after this her friend suddenly died. Within a year the patient started to have severe guilt feelings whenever she became angry with any other person, such as a co-worker at her place of employment. When she came for treatment she told the analyst that she had suffered from measles as a four-year-old child. Soon after, her little sister had also contracted measles and died. The parents locked up the surviving daughter in her room during the funeral and later accused her of passing her illness to her younger sister and thus killing her. They repeated this accusation on other occasions during the patient's developmental years. It was not difficult for an analyst to consider that in this case, the death of the baby sister, an external event, had induced an unconscious fantasy in the older sister, now a patient. While this individual was in analysis, the primary transference story centered on this pathological unconscious fantasy that she was a murderer.

In 1945 Otto Fenichel updated and summarized in depth Freudian psychoanalysis and its focus on the internal world of individuals in his well-known book, *The Psychoanalytic Theory of Neurosis*. In it he stated,

"The distinction between traumatic neuroses and psychoneuroses is an artificial one" (p. 541). The case vignette presented above fits Fenichel's statement well.

The avoided external events were the cultural, historical, and political ones. In 1943, Géza Róheim, an anthropologist and psychoanalyst, turned our attention to the importance of cultural issues in human psychology. In 1947, Edward Glower explored group psychology and its role in sadism, pacifism, and war. Erik Erikson (1950, 1959) became a key figure in exploring child-rearing practices and psycho-social development. He brought to our attention some cultural elements individuals in American Indian tribes experienced in their internal and external adjustment throughout different phases of life. Róheim's, Glower's, and Erikson's focus on large-group psychology and culture, however, did not substantially or quickly change the practice of "classical psychoanalysis" in the United States.

Beginning in the early 1950s, well-known psychoanalysts both in the US and Europe began to explore and write papers on a topic that became known as "the widening scope of psychoanalysis" (A. Freud, 1954; Jacobson, 1954; Stone, 1954; Weigert, 1954). John Frosch (1954) summarized Anna Freud's concerns on this subject:

> In the discussion [Arden House Conference, Harrison, May 1954] Anna Freud referred to analytic situations which evoked variations in technique. She regretted, however, what she felt was the enormous expenditure of time and energy involved in the treatment of borderline and psychotic cases in view of the small ultimate results. In her opinion it would be more rewarding to devote such efforts to less severe cases with greater therapeutic promise. (p. 565)

In spite of Anna Freud's remarks, however, individuals with what today we refer to as borderline or narcissistic personality organizations and other personality disorders, such as the one that expresses what I call "libidinal hunger" due to the person's early loss of love, continued to appear in psychoanalysts' offices. Eventually this would lead to psychoanalysts' writing about various new theories explaining such personality disorders and the technique for their treatment (Kernberg, 1975; Kohut, 1971; Volkan, 1976). Outside of considerations about new technical concepts and especially focus on countertransference responses, the widening scope of psychoanalysis resulted in attention to how such patients strongly and more openly react to the external events in their environments and often try to change them or at least perceive them according to their internal demands. The intertwining of external and internal worlds and also the role of historical, cultural, and political external events as key factors in psychopathology in general began to receive more attention. In the 1960s and 1970s there were significant contributions to studying history from a psychoanalytic angle and examining the inability to mourn after shared massive traumas at the hand of the Other (Fornari, 1966; Mitscherlich, 1971; Mitscherlich & Mitscherlich, 1973; Wolman, 1971).

By the 1970s, American, European, Israeli, and other psychanalysts' avoidance of recalling and re-experiencing the dreadful external world of the Nazi period to a great extent had begun fading away, and more and more studies of the influence of the Third Reich on the psyche of the survivors (victims and perpetrators) surfaced. (For a review of this literature see Brenner, 2014; Kestenberg & Brenner, 1996; Kogan, 1995; Laub & Auerhahn, 1993; Volkan, Ast, & Greer, 2002.) Psychoanalysts with a "classical" orientation began to realize that the specific nature of any given historical event is important when it symbolically becomes a mirror of our pre-oedipal or oedipal conflicts and our defenses against them. After detailed psychoanalytic work on Holocaust victims (for example: Krystal, 1968; Niederland, 1961, 1968), Sander Abend (1986) wrote that "[T]he impact of daily events, inner as well as outer plays upon our psychic integration and produces those fluctuations of mood, thought, and behavior which are part of our so-called normal personalities" (p. 565). He added that the analysand and the analyst are constantly affected by shifting internal and external events. He suggested that the analyst cannot simply remain as a pure and non-changing "analyzing instrument." In 1991, Jacob Arlow, who was a key figure among the architects of the ego psychology that dominated the American psychoanalytic scene in the 1960s and 1970s, wrote:

> I think it is a fair statement that psychoanalysts today consider many more factors that contribute to the shaping of the individual— dynamic, biological, adaptive, developmental, experiential, and cultural factors. Where they differ is in the relative emphasis they give to one or another of these elements. (p. 60)

Some decades after the Holocaust several Jewish psychoanalysts, such as Charlotte Kahn (2008), Emily Kuriloff (2013), Vera Muller-Paisner (2005),

Anna Ornstein (Ornstein & Goldman, 2004), Paul Ornstein (Ornstein & Epstein, 2015), and Henri Parens (2004), were ready to write about their own Holocaust-related traumatic experiences. German-speaking psychoanalysts, such as Anita Eckstaedt (1989), Ilse Grubrich-Simitis (1979), and Annette Streeck-Fischer (1999) have explored the difficulties of "hearing" and having empathy with Nazi-related influences in their German and Jewish patients. Eckstaedt brought overdue attention to the trauma that ethnic Germans themselves experienced during the Third Reich and to the influence of that trauma on the self-conception of contemporary Germans.

In 1997 and 1998 I was asked to work with a small group of ethnic German and Jewish-German analysts and therapists when they formed an organization to end "the silence" about the Holocaust-related issues that come up during clinical practice (Opher-Cohn, et al., 2000). After working with these colleagues in Germany, I realized that such a "silence" was real and that it was difficult to deal with (Volkan, 2015a; Volkan, Ast, & Greer, 2002). Nevertheless, the controversy among the members of the American Psychoanalytic Association about bringing the danger—resulting from authoritarian regimes, wars, war-like conditions, and political change—into the psychoanalytic focus would openly continue until the early 2000s (Brenner, 2002).

Meanwhile, beginning in the 1980s and spreading into the 1990s and 2000s, a new phenomenon occurred in psychoanalysis that became known as the "pluralistic landscape of psychoanalysis" (Samberg, 2004, p. 243). Several "schools" were put under the umbrella of "democracy in the field" and each one of them claimed to be psychoanalytic. Under this democratic approach, even some crucial classical concepts of psychoanalysis and psychoanalytic technique were questioned by some "schools." In certain circles, the new "psychoanalytic technique" seemed to place more focus on the patient's relationship with the external world in general—not necessarily the external world related to history, culture, and politics—and the psychoanalyst's "managing" the patient's life instead of trying to achieve an internal structural change in the patient. Some psychoanalysts have now begun exhibiting some resistance against examining the analysand's unconscious dynamics at the expense of focusing on the patient's relationships to his external world, bypassing the examination of the intertwining of the two—internal and external worlds—in a sophisticated fashion. Other psychoanalysts, of the tradition that what counts in a proper psychoanalytic practice is the analysis of the analysand's dynamic unconscious, continued to resist dealing with the influences of current or past cultural, historical, and political events, wars or war-like situations, and what influence the emergence of authoritarian regimes have on patients' internal worlds and on the analytic practice in general. However, recognition of such problems and their impact on societies—not necessarily on clinical practice with individuals—began to increase.

Otto Kernberg (1980, 2003a, 2003b) started looking at mass psychology and political violence through the analytic lens, Raphael Moses (1982) examined the Arab–Israeli conflict from a psychoanalytic point of view, and Michael Šebek (1992, 1994) studied societal responses to living under communism in Europe. Edward Shapiro, with an Anglican priest, Wesley Carr (1993) wrote about tools that allow people to maintain meaningful connections in a rapidly changing world, while Peter Loewenberg (1995) went back to the history of the Weimar Republic and emphasized its humiliation and economic collapse as major factors in creating shared personality characteristics among the German youth and their embrace of Nazi ideology. Exploring events from a psychoanalytic angle traversed the globe: Sudhir Kakar (1996) described the effects of Hindu–Muslim religious conflict in Hyderabad, India; Maurice Apprey (1993, 1998) focused on the influence of transgenerational transmission of trauma on African Americans and their culture; Marta Cullberg Weston (1997) conducted extensive research in Yugoslavia as it was collapsing, and Nancy Hollander (1997) explored events in South America.

After the September 11, 2001 tragedy various study groups under the sponsorship of the International Psychoanalytical Association (IPA) explored this topic as well. One was the Terror and Terrorism Study Group chaired by Norwegian analyst Sverre Varvin that lasted for several years, during which time it commissioned a volume of collected papers he and I edited (Varvin & Volkan, 2003). The writings in this volume by colleagues with Jewish and Arab backgrounds include references to countertransference issues as well as note blind spots concerning the situation in the Middle East and its effects on the internal worlds of people from affected groups. In this book Werner Bohleber (2003) from Germany described collective fantasies and terrorism. In other initiatives, the International Psychoanalytical Association Committee to the United Nations, which was established a year before the September 11 attacks, increased its activities. In 2017 the IPA envisioned that this UN Committee would continue to work as a separate committee for two more years, and that it will eventually be a subcommittee under the umbrella of the IPA and Humanitarian Organizations Committee. The theme of the 44th Annual Meeting of the IPA in Rio de Janeiro in the summer of 2005 was "trauma," including trauma due to historical events. Clearly, psychoanalytic studies covering massive external events in many parts of the world expanded greatly.

Psychoanalysts' exploration of world affairs almost became routine following September 11, 2001. Here I will only give examples of the psychoanalytic look at external world affairs after September 11 with which I am very familiar.

Mitch Elliott, Kenneth Bishop, and Paul Stokes (2004) from the Irish Institute of Psycho-Social Studies, referred, among other things, to the troubles in Northern Ireland and stated that, "In the world of psychoanalysis there has been a tendency, in addressing societal questions, to abandon the rigor of the consulting room, and to resort to a long-distance speculation" (p. 1). Interestingly, they asserted that social diversity "seriously affects what is considered 'normal' and what is deemed 'pathological.' Failure to address it may, moreover, contribute by counter-transference to the formation of psychoanalytic 'schools' antipathetic toward each other" (p. 14). John Alderdice (2007, 2010) also examined the situation in Northern Ireland.

Peter Olsson (2007, 2014) wrote about the cult of Osama bin Laden and the making of home-grown terrorists. Other studies examining the terrorist mind and the fundamentalist mind by psychoanalysts became available (Erlich, 2010; Strozier, Terman, and Jones, 2010), and Nancy Hollander (2010) described the impact of terrorism on Americans.

In Sweden Tomas Böhm and Susan Kaplan (2011) examined the theme of revenge in different cultures and religions. They looked at surviving psychic trauma by making references to the Holocaust and events in Rwanda, the former Yugoslavia, and other locations. In the United States Gerard Fromm (2011) explored transgenerational transmissions, and Salman Akhtar (2014) studied immigration, mourning, and adaptation. In Italy, Clara Mucci (2013) presented an impressive volume on subjective experience of trauma and examined mourning, creativity, forgiveness, and cultural processes following external traumatic events. During the last couple of years, the number of publications dealing with the psychodynamic aspects of similar topics continues to grow (for example, Alpert & Goren, 2017; Auestad et al., 2017; Hamburger, 2018; Hamburger & Laub, 2017; Keval, 2016; Naso & Mills, 2016; Ofer, 2017; Suistola & Volkan, 2017; Volkan, 2017) and the number of psychoanalysts, as well as other mental health workers, who have become involved in community affairs has also increased. Later in this book I will make references to my own studies of and findings about the various aspects of large-group psychology linked to history, culture, politics, and international relationships.

Attention paid to external world affairs would also influence psychoanalysts' clinical practice. One example of this comes from Ilany Kogan (1995, 2004) in Israel. With two detailed case reports, Kogan illustrated the role of the psychoanalyst in the analytic cure during times of chronic crises in Israel. In her first case, Kogan was able to stay with fears evoked in her patient by the traumatic external war-like situation. But, in her second case, for a long time she was like Melanie Klein treating Richard in World War II England. Kogan's blind focus on her patient's internal reality was an attempt to counteract her own sense of passivity and helplessness, as she, like her patient, was surrounded by chronic life-threatening elements in her external world. The psychoanalysis was being conducted when a chemical or biological attack on Israel was perceived to be imminent. Kogan made psychoanalytic interpretations of internal events, ignoring her own and her patient's fears. A turning point occurred when another important external event occurred. The psychoanalyst had a granddaughter. At that time, in Israel, parents of babies discharged from the hospital were given a little plastic bag. This, it was thought, would keep their newborn safe in case of a chemical or biological attack. Kogan envisioned what could happen during such an attack: young parents, her son and her daughter-in-law, wearing gas masks while frantically attempting to put the screaming baby into this device and then being unable to touch and calm her. This image made Kogan aware that she was not coping with the existing situation, broke her denial of the external danger, and in turn enabled her to deal with her patient's fears (2004).

My work on external world events and their impact on societies and individuals dates back to 1979. Besides writing about two ethnic groups in conflict in Cyprus, Cypriot Turks and Cypriot Greeks, and the human need to have large-group enemies and allies, as a psychoanalyst I also explored the Arab–Israeli conflict, Communism, events in the Baltic Republics after their independence following the collapse of the Soviet Union, the Serbian group-psychology after the collapse of the former Yugoslavia, the psychology of Romanians and Albanians following the death of dictators Nicolae Ceauşescu and Enver Hoxha, Kuwaiti responses to the invasion by Saddam Hussein's forces, the Georgian–South Ossetian conflict, the Turkish–Greek as well as Turkish–Armenian relationships, the psychology of extreme religious fundamentalism, the psychology of suicide bombers, refugee crises, and terrorism (1979, 1997, 2004, 2006, 2013, 2014a, 2017; Volkan & Itzkowitz, 1994; Volkan & Kayatekin, 2006; Suistola & Volkan, 2017).

In the next chapter I will describe the spread of psychoanalysis worldwide. Psychoanalytic teachers, mentors, and case supervisors working in foreign countries find it necessary to become familiar with cultural, historical, and political issues in these locations.

CHAPTER TWO

Teaching and Supervising Psychoanalytic Cases in a Foreign Country

D avid Sachs (2011) divided the spread of psychoanalysis into three roughly demarcated periods. During the first stage individuals obtained analysis from Sigmund Freud or one of his close collaborators and discussed their own cases with the "guru" and associates and formed psychoanalytic groups. The second stage started when the International Psychoanalytical Association (IPA) took over the establishment of societies in 1910 and evolved an agreed-upon training program. Sachs informs us that an entirely new stage developed due to two events in the late 1980s. First, a lawsuit was filed by four psychologists against the American Psychoanalytic Association. Although nonmedical applicants were accepted for training at psychoanalytic institutes outside of the US, until the lawsuit was settled in favor of the psychologists such applicants could not be trained in the American IPA-approved training programs. Around this time a second unexpected event took place—the Soviet Union collapsed. Psychoanalysis had existed in Russia beginning in the 1920s, but it was prohibited after 1936. With the collapse of communism in Russia and other locations, psychoanalytic training spread to former communist countries. This development obviously brought attention to historical, cultural, and political elements when analysts from Europe, the United States, Israel, and elsewhere began supervising cases of psychoanalytic candidates in foreign countries. The IPA-sponsored activities and other private organizations' efforts related to the spreading of psychoanalysis certainly brought increased attention to issues I examine in this book.

Jerome Blackman from Virginia Beach and David Scharff and Jill Scharff from Chevy Chase, Maryland have been teaching psychoanalysis in China for many years. From their first visits to China, these American psychoanalysts have considered themselves students of culture, history, and politics. Jerome Blackman (2018) shared with me his work with a Chinese psychotherapist. This psychotherapist's patient was a twenty-one-year-old male college student whose chief complaint was persistent anxiety about stepping on numbers or images. This began at puberty, when he was about thirteen and in middle school, when he particularly had a fear of stepping on the number four, which in Chinese is the word *si*, meaning death. The sounds are similar. He also had a fear of stepping on the number eight, which is exactly the same sound as the word for father—*ba*. These fears had influenced his life. Blackman learned that the patient is the second child in the family, with a sister who is four years his senior. Apparently, the patient's father's mother had pushed the father to have a son, a family "treasure." This was during the time of China's one-child policy, implemented by the Chinese government in 1979 in response to the country's explosive population growth, and so the family sent the daughter to the mother's sister to be raised. The mother then became pregnant with the patient and, according to what he was told while growing up, she almost died during pregnancy and risked punishment for even bearing him. Dr. Blackman inquired as to what the punishment would have been if the parents had been caught breaking the law in this way. He was informed that they both would have lost their jobs and probably would have been fined severely. In other words, there was a danger, in reality, that both of the patient's parents could have been punished if found out. Dr. Blackman later would find more connections between the patient's symptoms and his family story. It is clear that without some knowledge of the Chinese language and an understanding of the political situation that existed at that time, it would have been impossible to understand the Chinese psychotherapist's patient's psychology. When I learned that Blackman studied Chinese and learned to read and speak it, I became most appreciative of his dedication to teaching and mentoring in China.

David and Jill Scharff (2011) also provide examples of cultural and political elements influencing patients of Chinese psychotherapists they have supervised. They wrote: "Unconscious thought, fantasies, and actions of individuals as a group give form to the social system, and the social system affects the unconscious of the individuals in a cycle of mutual influence" (p. 83). David Scharff (2018) reminds us that the Chinese have a 2500-year history and loyalty to their large group. This history includes the teaching of Confucius that each person should be subservient to the large group, honoring the emperor, the family, and the father. Even though some cultural and political changes have taken place in China, valuing older sons above others and arranged marriages are still common. "Thus, the individualism we see in contemporary China is a conflictual one" (p. 12). He also informs us that Chinese thought is metaphorical. He gives an example by referring to Chairman Mao Zedong's statement, "Women hold up half the sky." Everybody knew that Mao was talking about the equality of women.

In another case, a thirty-six-year-old Japanese man who was living in the United States sought treatment from Gunther Perdigão because he was experiencing depression. Because the man's English was poor, Perdigão was concerned about bridging the cultural gap and wondered how one follows a patient's associations that are taking place in a language other than the analyst's mother tongue. He remembered that for many of Freud's patients, including the "Wolf Man," and Miss Lucy R., German was a second language. Perdigão analyzed this Japanese man—in English—four times a week over three years until his patient had to return to Japan. It is beyond my aim here to describe this patient's life story and problems, but I wish to point out that Perdigão (2018) learned what *amae* is and read some Japanese psychoanalysts' explanations of this feeling. From Perdigão I learned that *amae* is an important organizing principle in understanding the emotional life of Japanese people. For example, the patient would state that in Japan people do not express their desire or need directly in a relationship. He added, "When we drink sake, we pour the sake for others but not for ourselves." The analyst noted that what his patient was describing was in great contrast to the American "help yourself" attitude. His realization that his patient was expecting to intuit feelings without having to verbalize them helped in conducting the analysis.

Since I was born to Turkish parents on Cyprus, Turkish is my mother tongue. In 1932, the year I was born, there were about 350,000 souls on the island, which was a British colony. Two ethnic groups, Greeks and, in lesser numbers, Turks, lived next door to each other in the same cities, towns, and some villages. In other villages only Greeks or only Turks resided. The island is also home to smaller numbers of Armenians, Maronites, and some Phoenicians.

In 1950, at age eighteen, I went to Turkey to study medicine at the University of Ankara. To complete a medical school education in Turkey takes six years, and I graduated in June 1956. Eight months later I took part in a process known as the "brain drain," and came to the United States, speaking rather broken English. Apparently, in those days there was a shortage of physicians in the United States, and young physicians from many countries were encouraged to come and work there. I was never a citizen of Turkey and came to the United States as a British citizen. I ended up becoming an American citizen in the early 1960s, decided to stay, and went through my psychiatric as well as my psychoanalytic training in my new country.

In the 1950s Turkey was still progressing in its modernization and Westernization efforts, which began after the Republic was officially proclaimed on October 29, 1923, following the collapse of the Ottoman Empire. Kemal Atatürk, the first president of Turkey was my idealized godlike figure. He had died in 1938, but I had identified fully with his secularist and nationalist ideology. I was not involved in any religious activity, except culturally, celebrating some religious holidays without having any idea why such days were important. Two decades after my becoming an American citizen I went to Turkey for a year to study Atatürk's life and to write, with Princeton University historian Norman Itzkowitz, a psychobiography of this leader (Volkan & Itzkowitz, 1984). This allowed me to abandon my godlike image of Atatürk and see him as a human I much admired.

When I started treating American patients, in a sense, I was like Jerome Blackman, David Scharff, and Jill Scharff when they initiated their work in China, or Gunther Perdigão when he began analyzing a Japanese individual. I had to improve my English and learn various aspects of the United States' historical, cultural, and political issues. I appreciated the exceptional and glorified aspects of life in my new country. But I also learned about and felt the impact its history of slavery and racism had on American communities (Volkan, 2009). Since Cypriot Greeks had a different language, a different religion, and their children went to different schools than Cypriot Turkish children, I never had a Greek friend while growing up. But in Cyprus in those days there was no racism such as the kind I would witness later in the United States. While conducting psychoanalysis with Americans who belonged to rich white families in the American South, I came across individuals who were raised by "two mothers": one biological white mother and one black nanny. In their adulthood this situation would make an impact on their internalized self- and object relations and interpersonal relationships. Without knowing the American history of slavery and racism I would not have fully understood why these individuals could not integrate a "white mother" representation with a "black mother" representation and corresponding self-images devoted to two different "mothers" (Volkan, 2010; Volkan with Fowler, 2009).

As a psychoanalyst, I visit Turkey frequently and often give lectures at medical schools. About thirty years ago I felt embarrassed when I noticed that there was still no official International Psychoanalytical Association (IPA)-sponsored training for psychoanalysis in Turkey. As I have written about elsewhere, I worked hard and played a role in starting two IPA-approved psychoanalytic institutes in Istanbul (Volkan, 2011). Psychoanalytic teachers from Israel, Greece, France, the United States, and elsewhere began to develop these institutes. Then I received a letter from the IPA stating that I should not have a teaching position at these institutes. It stated that since I was of Turkish origin I might not be "neutral" in dealing with the students. I found this most ridiculous and wondered how psychoanalysts running the IPA, whom I would have liked to consider mature persons, could write such a letter. Nevertheless, as I did not want to jeopardize the IPA sponsorship of the new Turkish institutes, I stayed away from them in their developmental years. Then in the early 2000s things suddenly changed; I was invited to be involved in teaching and supervising the psychoanalytic candidates' work at one of the institutes. Retrospectively realizing their mistake, one high-level person from the IPA committee dealing with the Turkish institutes met me at an international meeting and indirectly apologized for the organization. I willingly began supervising psychoanalytic candidates in Istanbul.

I am aware that while establishing the psychoanalytic institutes in Turkey, the IPA tried to assign them teachers and supervisors who were familiar with the social customs, and political and historical events in that country. For example, two Turkish-speaking psychoanalysts with connections to Turkey, one from France and the other from Greece, were involved in the establishment of one of these institutes in Istanbul. However, other psychoanalysts with no deep knowledge of the foreign country where they would work had also become teachers and supervisors. But I felt good that I would supervise a few Turkish psychoanalytic candidates' cases, including the candidate who would start working with the businessman whose story I will introduce in the next chapter.

Selma Fraiberg, Edna Adelson, and Vivian Shapiro (1975) reminded us that, "In every nursery there are ghosts" (p. 387). They were referring to parents' own psychological traumas and problems. They described how such traumas and problems influence the parents' role in feeding, toilet training, disciplining, and in general raising their children, and also influence their interpretation of their infants' behavior. They added: "Even among families where the love bonds are stable and strong, the intruders from the parental past may break through the magic circle in an unguarded moment, and a parent and his child may find themselves reenacting a moment or a scene from another time with another set of characters" (p. 387).

Two years ago, Adrienne Harris, Margery Kalb, and Susan Klebanoff (2016a, 2016b) edited two books giving clinical examples of other types of ghosts and demons that interfere with the work of mourning. Their books provide accounts of unpredictable effects of trauma and explore unmetabolizable feelings related to loss on both an individual and mass scale, working through perennial mourning, and learning to move forward.

CHAPTER THREE

A Man Who Was Afraid of Ghosts and Graves

An Istanbul businessman was forty-seven years old and had been married for thirteen years when he started his analysis in the mid-2010s. During the previous ten years he had visited ten psychiatrists for his sexual problem: losing his erection most of the time as he would enter his wife's vagina. He needed to use drugs to deal with his erectile dysfunction. Some psychiatrists he consulted had also given him medication indicated for someone experiencing depression; others had suggested that he go to a gym, exercise and strengthen his muscles. In reality, he was taking good care of his body and had been an active member of a sports club. His visits to all these psychiatrists had not helped him.

One evening while dining with his wife at a restaurant, a group of people sitting at the next table were speaking rather loudly. One man who was about his age was describing how psychotherapy had changed his life, freed him from his previous social inhibitions, and made him more assertive. The next day while in his office, the businessman had an impulse. He buzzed his secretary and asked her to find the names of a few good psychotherapists in Istanbul. A few hours later the secretary presented him with the names of four psychotherapists. He chose the first name, the name of a female psychiatrist, called and made an appointment.

This businessman's eleventh psychiatrist happened to be a psycho-analytic candidate in training whom I had met during a visit to Istanbul.

She had been looking for her second analytic case to be conducted under supervision, as required for her education. I became her supervisor, and we began our consultation on the phone once a week, with face-to-face meetings whenever I visited Istanbul.

The patient's first name in Turkish suggests someone who has great strength. Because of this, here I will call him Mert, which in Turkish means "manly." I never asked for his last name, and his analyst never mentioned it. Therefore, I do not know who this person is. I also wish to protect the analyst's identity. Let us call her Dr. Ufuk.

During the initial session with her patient, Dr. Ufuk learned that Mert was the owner of a factory that employed hundreds of workers producing construction material for new buildings and roads. He also owned a medium-size four-star hotel in Istanbul. She noted that Mert was a tall and handsome man with blond hair and blue eyes. However, he did not impress her as manly or successfully rich. Mert hung his head and seemed afraid to stand upright. Dr. Ufuk, who is younger than the patient, perceived forty-seven-year-old Mert as an anxious child.

Mert told Dr. Ufuk that he had been born and raised in an isolated farmhouse on the eastern Black Sea coast of Turkey, a few kilometers away from a village where his relatives lived. His parents were uneducated. His father had goats and cows, raised tea plants, and had dozens of beehives producing honey. Mert had two sisters, one four years older and one three years younger than him. He recalled that his father paid little attention to his children while they were growing up because he was so busy with his farm work, animals, and beehives. Mert described his mother as an anxious person. She cooked, entertained relatives whenever they came to the farm, and had the primary responsibility for raising the children. She also worked on the farm and often left her children alone in the farmhouse. She would ask her oldest child to look after the younger ones when an older relative was unavailable to care for them.

After Mert was born, his two aunts who visited the farm often declared that Mert had a small penis. As Mert was growing up, his aunts' perception of his penis size was kept as a "reality" in his mind. He described how he slept with his siblings on a big bed until he was twelve years old. He did not report seeing parents' sexual activities or any sexual involvement with his siblings. As a Muslim child Mert had been circumcised. Years ago, the Turkish psychiatrist and academician Orhan Öztürk and I (Öztürk & Volkan, 1971) wrote about circumcision of boys in Turkey, especially in villages.

> Circumcision of boys is done without anesthesia, usually between the ages of four and eight. Because of many compensatory and counterphobic factors such as verbal preparations, ceremonies, gifts, the enhancement of the masculinity status, and so on, this potentially traumatic operation becomes something strongly needed by the ego, so much so that the lack of it may be severely traumatic. (p. 249)

Mert had only very vague memories of his circumcision that took place at age four. Apparently, he had gone through this religious tradition along with some male cousins. He remembered the male crowd applauding the circumcised boys and giving them gifts. As a patient he did not think of his circumcision as a traumatic event, and he did not connect this event with his thinking of his penis as small.

What he did report was his childhood fear of ghosts. His mother took him to a village *hodja*, a "priest" of the Moslem religion, for advice and help for his ghost phobia. Many *hodjas*, especially in villages,

> ... have no religious training or function but are able to find a means of introducing themselves as men of religion and wisdom; they use a good deal of quackery. Their practices are rather stereotyped in that they inscribe amulets, pray, breathe, or lay their hands on patients, massage, pray to the water, and offer it as a conjured drink. (Öztürk & Volkan, 1971, p. 260)

The village *hodja* gave little Mert a religious amulet (a *muska*) to protect the boy from ghosts. He carried this amulet around his neck for many years.

Mert recalled being awakened early in the morning in order to walk to the elementary and later to the middle school in the village. He described, without detail, being beaten by a girl in the elementary school. Mert entered a high school in a nearby town, about ten kilometers from the village, where he stayed by himself most of the time. He recalled only eating dark bread and cheese and being afraid of a cat. Once a teacher spanked him. He did not recall the details of this event but remembered that it embarrassed him badly. When not attending school, Mert also worked on the farm while he was growing up. Sometimes he would injure himself while cutting tea leaves to be sold. He recalled his legs bleeding and this scaring him.

The sexual life of a teenager where Mert lived was restricted since free dating was not approved of by society. When he was seventeen years old he was swimming in the Black Sea bordering the town where he was attending high school. Some women were relaxing on the beach. When he came to shore a *jandarma*, a member of the Turkish National Police who are in charge of keeping peace in the countryside, approached him, shook him badly, and shouted at him. He felt extremely humiliated in front of his friends who were with him at the beach and the women watching who approved of what the *jandarma* was doing. The *jandarma* ordered Mert not to swim at this particular location. Apparently, the women at the beach had called the police and complained that young Mert had been watching them and implied that he was sexually abusing them. Mert had done no such thing. Nevertheless, he had been accused by the women of doing something that was culturally unacceptable in this part of the country, and it left him feeling extremely humiliated, scared, and traumatized.

The culture Mert grew up in supported "extended family" customs. The women at the beach did not belong to Mert's extended family. He was humiliated by women belonging to a different extended family or families. Let me diverge and describe what I know about such family structures at the time Mert was growing up, the late 1960s to the 1980s. The tradition-based agrarian population in Turkey was in a process of change as communication media were becoming more available. There was no doubt that after the Turkish Republic was established in 1923, its founder and first president Kemal Atatürk's revolution to secularize the state had been successful, but outside a minority circle of intellectual people, Islam still remained, at least as a "soft" ideology. The multiparty system and free elections since 1945 had brought into focus problems associated with the religious sentiments of the people. In 1946 only eleven religious associations and teaching institutions existed in Turkey. By the time of Mert's birth, in 1968, this figure had risen to 14,239 (Öztürk & Volkan, 1971). When Mert spoke to Dr. Ufuk about his childhood he did not indicate he had been forced to follow certain religious customs. However, as I already described above, he had been taken to a *hodja* for help in dealing with his fear of ghosts, and he wore a religious amulet around his neck for many years. I also learned that at age sixteen, with his mother's urging, he visited another *hodja* who gave him another amulet to protect him from ghosts, which he also wore for several years. Mert's description of his family during his diagnostic sessions with Dr. Ufuk indicated that it was a traditional unit with a primary emphasis on kinship ties.

In 2001 I received a grant from the International Research & Exchanges Board (IREX), an international, nonprofit organization that specializes in global education and development, to study gender issues and family violence in the Black Sea and Caspian Sea regions. Colleagues from Georgia, Turkey, Abkhazia, South Ossetia, and Armenia, and one person from Sweden joined me in this project. Our aim was to draw profiles of victims and perpetrators of family violence and focus on the cultural barriers to examining family violence, especially violence directed towards women and children in the above locations. The project's longer-term goals were to encourage further collaborative research in the Black Sea and Caspian Sea regions, to aid in the development of multidisciplinary task forces and/or organizations to bring victims' painful experiences and cultural dilemmas to public awareness, and to generally increase open public discussions of family violence-related issues (Volkan et al., 2002).

Family violence occurs in every society around the globe, including American society. At the time we carried out the above project, psychoanalytic literature studying antecedents associated with family violence and abuse included the following in an abuser: lack of an early nurturing environment, early childhood traumas and humiliations (Kramer & Akhtar, 1991; Levine, 1990; Rothstein, 1984; Shengold, 1989), and development of character traits in which aggressive and sexual acts are experienced as temporarily enhancing the subject's self-esteem (Kernberg, 1984; Volkan & Ast, 1994). After studying eighteen cases in the Black Sea and Caspian Sea regions we noted that these cases were no different in their individualized qualitative factors for behavioral outcomes than cases from the US or Sweden. What took on particular importance for our research was the focus upon location-specific cultural and societal factors that either increased or reduced the likelihood of family violence. The most prominent findings related to societal factors as precursors to family violence, especially the influence exerted by threats, including ethnic wars, migrations from rural areas to urban areas, and poverty, and the existing extended family structure in all locations studied. Traditional extended family structure, by itself, does not cause family violence or dysfunction. In a stable society, the extended family provides protection, support, and rituals that keep individual anxiety in check and serves as a source of continuous identity. Here I will describe some key characteristics of an extended family without reference to variations in cultural and social customs within the locations studied.

In an extended family, one family name (the bride receives the groom's family name) identifies a number of different individuals, all of whom are supposed to have recognizable family characteristics—behavioral as well as physical—in common. Some families have a reputation for generosity, for example, and others for greed. Members are expected to refrain from asserting individual deviance from the family style. They share one another's emotional, social, and economic problems, presenting a united front to the world. However, there is always the potential for intra-family violence. Uncertainty concerning the boundaries dividing one member from another tends to engender aggression. If the extended family structure is functioning well and every member knows his or her role, then aggression is either channeled or suppressed. However, if the extended family structure is threatened, then violence may erupt.

According to the cultural norms at the locations in our study, if a wife does not produce a male child for her husband, her status within the extended family may be degraded and her husband may take additional "wives" or lovers in order to produce a male heir. Although on the surface the extended Turkish families are male-dominated, a closer examination revealed that the mother of the male head of the family is usually the one who determines the emotional climate. An old Turkish expression states, for example, that: "Heaven and Hell lie at the feet of the mother." The mother-in-law may also openly compete against her daughter-in-law by creating new family alliances against this "new" woman whom she perceives as a threat to her dominance.

Mert did not report any physical violence by his parents directed to their children. He did not recall fights between his mother and her mother-in-law who often took care of Mert and his siblings when Mert's mother was working on the farm. However, he was very aware of the importance of being a member of an extended family. While he was growing up he had noticed some dysfunction among different sections of his extended family. At this time Dr. Ufuk did not have detailed information about problems within Mert's extended family.

Mert left the Black Sea coast at age seventeen and went to Ankara, the capital city of Turkey, where he would study at a school to prepare him for a university entrance examination. Dr. Ufuk did not have an opinion about why this uneducated family was keen to send their son away to become an educated person. Mert recalled how his father waved to him when he was leaving the village on a bus. This remained in his mind as the only and most important event illustrating his father's love for his son.

The population of Ankara today is more than four and a half million. When Mert went there the population was a little over two million. His father never visited him while he was in Ankara. Once he witnessed the father of one of his classmates visiting his son, and both the father and son were having a great time. Then he noticed that his classmate joined his father at a dinner table, drinking alcohol in front of his father. Mert was shocked. He could never imagine being friendly with his own father as his classmate was with his, and it would have been impossible for him to dare use alcohol in front of his own father.

When Mert was growing up on the eastern Black Sea coast of Turkey in the late 1970s, political violence accompanied by an economic crisis was a big problem. Between 1976 and 1980 more than 5,000 people lost their lives in this country divided between leftist and rightist groups. A military coup took place in September 1980, and a military government assumed power until the November 1987 elections. When Mert went to Ankara these demoralizing troubles seemed to be over, but the impact of the leftist–rightist dilemma would still have been felt.

As a university student in Ankara, Mert was involved in leftist political protests. This was not surprising. While attending high school in the town near his family farm he had become aware of how many individuals on the eastern Black Sea coast had turned to radical forms of Marxism. In spite of his participation in the protests, Mert declared that he was socially shy and did not have steady girlfriends. He had his first sexual relation with a prostitute when he was twenty years old. At that time, sex work in Turkey was legal and regulated. There was a brothel near the old Ankara Castle where men over eighteen could enter through a metal gate after showing their identification card to a police officer and visit one of the houses where prostitutes worked from 10 a.m. to 10 p.m. In early 2013, Turkey cracked down on legal brothels and they were closed. Mert had gone to the gated brothel with a classmate who had visited this place twice before. When he entered one of the houses there were four sex workers that he could choose between and then go to a room and have intercourse with her. Mert recalled not choosing a young and beautiful sex worker, but instead choosing a middle-aged one with wrinkled skin. He managed to enter this woman but had a premature ejaculation. He could not enjoy the experience, and felt humiliated and scared.

Mert confessed to Dr. Ufuk that he had received help from another student for his university graduation examination. He graduated and received a diploma for agricultural studies, but apparently he felt that his diploma was a fake one since he had cheated by getting help from his friend. When Mert was informing Dr. Ufuk about seeing ten psychiatrists before becoming her patient he said: "I finished the university, but I knew I had other things that I needed to finish." After receiving his diploma, he considered pursuing an academic career, but not at a location near his family home. Instead, by using his family money, he became a salesman of building materials. He moved to Istanbul, where he opened a small factory producing bricks in a poor section of this big city. As the years passed, his factory became a huge operation. He began selling all kinds of materials for building houses, skyscrapers, shopping malls, roads, and bridges. Eventually he bought a hotel, renovated it and became very rich. Mert's younger sister moved to Istanbul as well, and her husband who also belonged to Mert's extended family became a junior partner at the factory. His older sister married a relative in the village and remained there.

At age thirty-three, Mert met his future wife. She had a junior managerial role at his factory. She was a "city girl" from a middle-class family in Istanbul. He dated his future wife for only four months before they were married. He had not told his family living on the Black Sea coast of his intention to marry; he was afraid they would not approve of his marrying a city girl. His wife was fourteen years younger than him and a virgin. When he came to see Dr. Ufuk, the couple's only child, a son, was twelve years old.

Mert recalled having a panic attack during his first intercourse with his wife and having a premature ejaculation. Starting very early in his marriage he began taking medication to correct his erectile dysfunction and exercised daily in order to maintain his physical manliness. He declared that there was a "wall" between him and his wife but could not explain the nature of it.

Mert told Dr. Ufuk that he, his wife, and son were living in a big house with a garden in a high-class section of Istanbul. He also described how he and his wife were overprotecting their son. Their son began sleeping in a bed with his teddy bear, most likely a "transitional object" (Winnicott, 1953), in his parents' bedroom five years prior to Mert's consultation with Dr. Ufuk. Mert and his wife were afraid that someone might kidnap their son if he slept alone in another room. This arrangement had caused the couple practically to stop any sexual activity between them. The family had a maid and other people helping them, but these individuals did not stay in the house overnight.

This information about Mert became available to Dr. Ufuk during her eighth session with the patient after meeting with him once or twice a week. At this point Dr. Ufuk made an initial formulation explaining Mert's erectile dysfunction and character trait of having an unmanly demeanor. Dr. Ufuk focused on Mert's possible psychological reactions to supposedly having a "small penis," his not having "good enough" parenting (Winnicott, 1965), and his sleeping with his siblings. At the farmhouse they did not have a bathroom. Family members would bathe in the kitchen about once a month. Until he was twelve years old his mother would come to the kitchen while Mert was bathing and rub his back with a sponge. Dr. Ufuk considered the possibility her patient could have been exposed to sexuality at home and how such a situation could unconsciously stimulate incestuous fantasies that might lead to sexual inhibitions. Mert had chosen to describe to his eleventh psychiatrist the traumatic event at age seventeen when he was accused of looking at women on a beach and being humiliated for this reason. He also spoke of his choosing an older sex worker for his first sexual encounter and then experiencing this encounter also as a traumatic event.

Dr. Ufuk imagined that Mert had difficulty moving up on his psychosexual developmental ladder, completing successfully his separation–individuation phase (Mahler, Pine, & Bergman, 1975), and passing successfully through his oedipal phase. Mert's father was a distant father; Mert had recalled only one event when his father showed his affection for him openly, when he was leaving for Ankara. Dr. Ufuk thought that Mert was stuck in an oedipal struggle. Her patient might be "castrating" himself by his erectile dysfunction. On the other hand, by using his business skills he was achieving superiority over his father. However, he would "hide" his success by appearing like a scared child. To be at a high place—to be number one at his business—was accompanied by a phobia of high places. Dr. Ufuk thought that it was now time to ask Mert to begin lying on her analytic couch so they could slowly start exploring Mert's difficulties in his psychosexual development and work toward helping him go through the passage of the oedipal phase successfully. Certainly, the patient had "other things he needed to finish." I agreed with Dr. Ufuk.

When she met with Mert again she told him that his going through psychoanalysis would be the best response to find solutions to his problems. She described how they would work together if he agreed to come and lie on her couch four times a week. He wanted to think about this offer because it would take a great deal of time from his work, even beyond the four hours, due to Istanbul's horrible daytime traffic.

Dr. Ufuk continued to meet with the patient face to face twice a week while waiting for Mert to decide to go through psychoanalysis. During this time, he mostly talked about his phobia of ghosts and his fear of seeing graves. His childhood phobias continued. Whenever he visited his village and passed by a graveyard he would imagine dead people emerging from the graves. He recalled passing through a graveyard as he walked to and from his middle school, even during the winter in the snow, and always having anxiety. Now he wanted Dr. Ufuk to know that in fact he had three siblings. When he was eleven years old, passing through his adolescence, his mother delivered another baby, a male sibling. But this baby died when he was ten months old. Mert gave details of how his father and other male extended family members dug a grave in the garden just in front of their house and buried the dead baby. Mert recalled the image of the dead brother wrapped in a white cloth before his burial and watching the burial and his crying mother. He wondered if he started to have grave and ghost phobias after this event. Yet, he knew that his phobias had started earlier in his childhood. He recalled having repeated dreams of dead people coming back to life long before his baby brother's birth and death.

Soon Dr. Ufuk and I would learn that Mert's phobia of ghosts had another connection than his exposure to the burial of his baby brother and his mother's grief. He said: "I did not know how to speak Turkish until I was seven years old." Apparently he began learning Turkish only after he started going to elementary school. He said that at home everyone spoke a different language. He went on to tell Dr. Ufuk how he learned for the first time at age nineteen when he was already in Ankara what language he spoke as a child. One day, on a bus, he was speaking with his roommate who was from his village, using their original childhood language. Hearing them, a man turned to them and said: "You are not Turkish! You are speaking Armenian." According to Mert, this was the first time he had recognized that he was "an Armenian assimilated within the general Turkish population." He referred to himself as a "Muslim Armenian." Soon after learning that his childhood language was Armenian he went to his village and told his parents about what had happened on the bus. He asked them if they considered themselves to be Armenians. His parents became very upset and told him they were Turks. But Mert began wondering about his ancestors, the Hemshin people, the Armenians who were Islamicized in the seventeenth and eighteenth centuries but preserved their language. They were ghosts from his past!

CHAPTER FOUR

The Beginning of Analysis and Therapeutic Neutrality

Mert found a solution to beginning his psychoanalytic process. His office was on the first floor of his hotel. I imagined that his phobia of high places prohibited him from having an office on the top floor. The hotel was next door to a metro station, and he had noticed a metro station next to Dr. Ufuk's office. As he had a car and driver, he did not recall the last time he had used the metro to travel within the city. Now he was willing to do so to reach Dr. Ufuk's office quickly. His wife apparently was tired of him seeing one psychiatrist after another and told him not to trust medical people, so he told her that he would see the new therapist only once week. Instead he started to come to Dr. Ufuk's office for analysis four times a week and use her couch.

During the first hour of his psychoanalysis Mert asked Dr. Ufuk if he should take off his shoes and jacket before lying on the couch. She did not tell him what to do but stated that they would wonder about his request and see if there might be some meanings attached to it. Mert took off his shoes and jacket before lying on the couch. His first story that day was about taking his shoes off and swimming in the Black Sea and being afraid of meeting a shark. His taking off his shoes and his jacket as if he were going to bed before using Dr. Ufuk's couch and his referring to the possibility of meeting a shark most likely reflected his expectations of facing some danger that existed from his childhood years coming up during his analysis and his perception of Dr. Ufuk as a transference figure who might hurt him. The analyst did not tell her new analysand what came to her mind. She would wait to hear what would be associated with such expectations.

One reason surfaced explaining Mert's urgency to seek psychiatric help for the eleventh time. As I stated above, for five years he and his wife were afraid of someone kidnapping their son. Five years earlier, the daughter of one of Mert's cousins in his village, without the permission of her parents, had left home and joined a young man from another extended family with the idea that they would soon get married. However, the young man's extended family did not accept the girl. Meanwhile the young woman could not return to her family's home because she had dishonored her extended family. A feud started between the two extended families, both of Hemshin descent. Mert arranged for the young woman, the cause of this trouble, to come to his house in Istanbul. For about a year, until other arrangements were made, this woman stayed in Mert's house. Mert's wife did not like this situation, and she did not develop a close relationship with her husband's relative staying under the same roof. Meanwhile, she and Mert felt that someone from the village, from Mert's extended family, might try to kidnap their son to punish them for protecting a relative who had hurt the family's honor. Now four years had passed since the woman who had dishonored the family name had left their house. The patient wanted his son, who seemed to have no close friends, to no longer sleep in his parents' bedroom. This would mean that he could be freer to have a sexual relationship with his wife. But, would he be successful? He declared: "My wife is glued to our son. She does not want our son to sleep in another bedroom." Facing or not facing his erectile dysfunction and related issues had become hot again. This played a big role in his seeking the eleventh psychiatrist. Dr. Ufuk listened to her new analysand without giving any advice.

The next session, Mert did not take off his shoes and jacket before lying on the psychoanalytic couch. As soon as he lay down he said: "Now, I am looking at myself from another window!" He became very aware that the psychoanalytic process would be different than therapeutic responses given to him by the previous ten psychiatrists. He talked about a dream he had the night before. Dr. Ufuk noted how Mert was an intelligent person who had already picked up on how psychoanalysts are interested in their patients' dreams after noticing his analyst's response to his relating repeated dreams of his childhood about ghosts and graveyards.

In the dream someone was attempting to take away Mert's university diploma. Once more he referred to his "fake" diploma. He recalled the occasion when a stranger thought of him as German because of his blond hair and blue eyes. His associations quickly went to his first learning that he was an ethnic Armenian when he was already nineteen years old. He told his analyst that since starting his analysis he was trying to learn more about his ancestors. The night before he had his dream he had researched Hemshin people on Google. "You learn everything right away," he added. Dr. Ufuk thought that Mert's dream reflected how he also thought of himself as a "fake" Turk. Mert might be wondering how his analyst, who was not a Hemşinli, would react to him. She did not share what had come to her mind, waiting to see what else her patient would say.

After a brief silence, in a soft voice, Mert began to speak in his "Hemshin language," sounding as if he were crying. He translated what he was saying: "There is a Hemşinli Association in Istanbul. This association's aim is to carry our old culture to new generations. I know some of its members. They belong to the rightist political party in Turkey praising and protecting Turkishness." He informed his analyst that this association was having a Hemşinli night to celebrate their culture. The patient had been invited to attend. But when his wife refused to go to this event Mert did not participate in the celebration either. He added: "I am not Turkish. You cannot buy someone's identity." Then he began singing a song in his childhood language while crying. When he finished his song, he said to his analyst: "You made me sing a song!" The session ended.

I already mentioned that at the beginning of her work with Mert, Dr. Ufuk did not know much about individuals in Turkey who call themselves Hemşinli. When I was attending medical school in Ankara during the first half of the 1950s I might have known something about them, but if so, I had completely forgotten it. When Dr. Ufuk started to work with Mert I had no idea of the existence of the Hemshin people. I had a classmate who was a Laz person from the eastern Black Sea area of Turkey where, as I now know, an estimated 150,000 Hemşinli are also located. The estimated number of Laz people in present-day Turkey ranges from half a million to one and a half million. Historians tell us that they are descendants of the Colchis, the people of an ancient kingdom that ethnically belong to a Katvelian-speaking branch of the Georgians. Ottomans conquered the area where the Laz lived in 1547. Some Laz people became Muslims, and as centuries passed they evolved as Turks. The Laz who stayed in Georgia remained Christian and merged their identity with the Georgians. I never considered my Laz class-mate as someone belonging to a minority group. He was a Turk from the Black Sea coast, and I was a Turk from Cyprus.

Historians tell us that the Hemshin people were members of the Armenian Apostolic Church. The Seljuk Turks defeated the Byzantine Empire in 1071 at the Battle of Manzikert and ended the Byzantine author-ity in Anatolia and Armenia. At the end of the thirteenth century the Ottoman Empire replaced the Seljuk Empire, and in the fifteenth century the region where the Hemshin people lived was incorporated into the Ottoman Empire. By the seventeenth and eighteenth centuries some of the Hemshin people converted to Sunni Islam; others remained Christian and migrated elsewhere. When the Ottoman Empire collapsed, the present-day Turkish Republic was born and the "Muslim Armenians," still using their language, continued to live on the eastern Black Sea coast of the new Turkey.

Since I knew the Turkish language and culture, I felt I was an ideal super-visor for younger analysts in Istanbul with whom I had started to work. But now, supervising Dr. Ufuk's case, in a sense I had become a "foreigner," since for me the analysand belonged to a group about whom I had no knowledge. Being involved in Mert's psychoanalysis would bring to my mind memories of my relationship with Christian Armenians, memories I will report later as Mert's story unfolds.

Throughout many decades I have been a supervisor or a consultant for younger analysts in the United States, Turkey, Finland, Germany, and Russia. As a consultant or supervisor, I do not behave as a therapist. I do not delve into finding out and understanding the psychological issues of those who are my supervisees or who consult with me, unless they volunteer to open up. I wondered about Dr. Ufuk's background, her ethnic involvement, and her ability to protect her therapeutic neutrality.

When she started treating Mert in the mid-2010s, Turkey had changed in major ways. An authoritarian regime was making attempts to modify the Turkish identity—as it had been evolving after Kemal Atatürk's moderniza-tion revolutions following the collapse of the Ottoman Empire—and make it a more Islamic one. There seemed to be a trend to recreate old Ottoman customs. Minor and major religious differences within the Turkish popula-tion were exaggerated. The country also was dealing with the terrorist activ-ities of Partiya Karkerên Kurdistan (PKK, the Kurdistan Workers' Party). PKK was founded in Turkey in 1978, originally as a leftist organization—a politically ideological one based on a Marxist–Leninist model. In 1984 PKK announced a Kurdish uprising. Since then tens of thousands have been killed because of this Turkish–Kurdish conflict due to terrorism-related events and the Turkish military's response. Millions of Kurds in Turkey, many of them peaceful citizens, had no choice but to be aware of their ethnic identity as Kurds every day of their lives. Ethnic Turks, too, due to repeated tragic events, were also exposed daily to what had become known as the "Kurdish question" in the country and therefore were also aware of ethnic issues on a daily basis. Around this time, whenever I went to Turkey to speak at conferences I was aware of my hosts telling me who was Turkish; who was Kurdish; who belonged to another ethnic group; who was a Sunni Muslim in favor of changing the Turkish identity and making it more religious; who was an Alevi, another sect of Islam; who was a Jewish Turk, and who was a secular person who was afraid of what was happening in Turkey. I did not know Dr. Ufuk's background. Could she maintain her therapeutic neutrality while her new analysand was bringing hot ethnic issues to her office? I knew that she was still undergoing her own training analysis. If she was giving a personal response to her patient I suspected that she would discuss this issue with her own analyst.

Sigmund Freud mentioned "neutrality" for the first time (1915a) while referring to psychoanalysts' attitude toward their patients. The German word he used for it, as Alex Hoffer (1985) and Ernest Wallwork (2005) remind us, was "*Indifferenz*," not "*Neutralität*," the actual word for "neutrality." While translating Freud's works into English, James Strachey used the word "neutrality," thereafter replacing "indifference" as the term accepted in the English psychoanalytic literature. Freud's different comments regarding his stance on and the meaning of neutrality "focus upon specific technical problems," and when these comments are "taken in isolation" they do not adequately give a clear-cut understanding of what he meant by "neutrality" (Moore & Fine, 1990, p. 127). In 1919, however, Freud stressed that analysts should avoid turning a patient seeking our help "into our private property, to decide his fate for him, to force our own ideals on him, and with the pride of a Creator to form him in our own image and to see that it is good" (1919a, p. 164).

As one might expect, Freud's meaning has been discussed throughout the decades by many psychoanalysts from different schools of psychoanalysis (see for example: Adler & Bachant, 1996; Agatsuma, 2014; Bornstein, 1983; Gill, 1994; Glower, 1955; Greenson, 1958; Kernberg, 1976;

Klautau & Coelho, 2013; Kris, 1982; Laplanche & Pontalis, 1973; T. Shapiro, 1984; Stone, 1961). Anna Freud (1936) described neutrality in structural theoretical terms as meaning a stance equidistant from the demands of the id, ego, and superego. In later years, this interpretation was criticized, especially by ego psychologists who perceived psychoanalysts to be on the side of the patients' ego, with a goal of helping patients enrich it. Rachel Blass (2003) and Ernest Wallwork (2005) examined therapeutic neutrality from an ethical point of view. Nancy Hollander (2009) reminded us of "ethical non-neutrality" when psychoanalysts need to address global destructive processes; she was not however speaking about neutrality in the clinical setting.

Linking the concept of "neutrality" with the concept of "countertransference" took some time to develop; the reason for this will be described below. *Psychoanalytic Terms and Concepts* edited by Burness Moore and Bernard Fine in 1990 describes neutrality as it is perceived, in general, by today's practicing psychoanalysts, including me, and links it to countertransference:

> Central to psychoanalytic neutrality are keeping the countertransference in check, avoiding the imposition of one's own values upon the patient, and taking the patient's capacities rather than one's own desires as a guide .... The analyst's neutrality is intended to facilitate the development, recognition, and interpretation of the transference neurosis and to minimize distortions that might be introduced if he or she attempts to educate, advise, or impose values upon the patient based on the analyst's countertransference. (p. 127)

The concept of countertransference was first described by Freud (1910d), illustrating a patient's influence on the analyst's unconscious. In 1945 Otto Fenichel published *The Psychoanalytic Theory of Neurosis*. In the 1960s and 1970s Fenichel's book was still among the best sources for a very detailed description of the updated version of classical psychoanalysis. In it Fenichel mentioned countertransference only once, negatively, by referring to an analyst's inability to analyze a patient with certain personality organizations. He suggested that under such circumstances the analyst should be analyzed more thoroughly. Ella Sharpe (1950) joined Fenichel in stating that the appearance of countertransference illustrates how an analyst is not sufficiently analyzed.

The history of the beginning of psychoanalysis, I believe, provides us with a reason why countertransference was perceived as an unwanted element within the analyst–patient relationship and why its int relationship was seen as a spoiler of therapeutic neutrality. In I described how replacing the sexual seduction of children as in the external world with stimuli that come from the child's own fantasies for the formation of psychopathology became a key focus of the new science called psychoanalysis. I also referred to the role the Sigmund Freud–Sándor Ferenczi dispute played in pioneer psychoanalysts placing less emphasis on the external world during psychoanalytic treatment. I believe that an analyst's countertransference feelings were considered as external to what is included in a patient's internal world. Experiencing and acknowledging such feelings were perceived by classical psychoanalysts as an intrusion into their therapeutic neutrality, thus preventing them from fully understanding the patient's internal world.

When I was training to be a psychoanalyst in the late 1960s, psychoanalysts in the United States still did not speak much about countertransference. If we talked about and illustrated our countertransference manifestations we were afraid they would show our unanalyzed infantile desires and defense mechanisms against them, and we might need to go through further analysis. Later, countertransference would receive increased attention (Searles, 1979). Two developments in psychoanalysis were the main reasons for this: (1) scientific research on the development of a child's mind, and (2) the widening scope of psychoanalysis accompanied by psychoanalytic pluralism.

Scientific observations of infants during the last few decades have informed us that an infant's mind is more active than we previously thought and have illustrated the existence of a psychobiological potential for "we-ness" and the role of child–mother/caregiver relationships in the development of the child's mind (see for example: Bloom, 2010; Brazelton & Greenspan, 2000; Cheour et al., 2002; Emde, 1991; Fonagy & Target, 1996; Greenspan, 1981; Lappi et al., 2007; Lehtonen, 2016; Purhonen et al., 2005; Stern, 1985). The functional independence of a child's environment and genes has been outdated (Kandel, 1998). We can no longer imagine an "autistic phase" (Mahler, 1968) in a baby's life. The fact that a child's internal world does not start developing without interactions with the mother and/or the other mothering persons was reflected in the analysts' offices. Stephen Seligman (2018) writes: "The infant developmentalists' assertion that relationships were primary, dislocated the instinct model's assumptions about infancy and, correspondingly, about the instinctual–primitive core of human psychology, child development, psychic structure, psychopathology, and clinical technique" (p. 99). An individual's analysis does not progress without taking into consideration that there are two persons in the analyst's office and that the transference–countertransference evolution is a necessary part of the patient's psychoanalytic process (Volkan, 2010). When this evolution interferes with the analyst's neutrality it has to be understood and dealt with in a therapeutic way.

In Chapter One I also described the widening scope of psychoanalysis accompanied by psychoanalytic pluralism and the benefits and pitfalls of this process. While working with a younger generation of psychoanalysts during the last few decades, I often noted their investment in this or that "school" of psychoanalytic thought, and I was puzzled by a stubborn "competition" among them.

When Dr. Ufuk first told me about her initial formulation about her patient's problems, the reader will notice she was only focusing on Mert's internal world, his possible unconscious fantasies and oedipal issues. Now her patient emotionally was introducing his large-group identity issues while on her couch. Dr. Ufuk told me how she was emotionally very moved when she heard Mert singing in Armenian while crying. Soon I would appreciate how she was a most capable therapist who could keep her therapeutic neutrality and develop empathy for Mert.

CHAPTER FIVE

Large-Group Identity

Before I continue describing what happened to Mert during his psychoanalysis I need to answer the following question: What is an ethnic, national, or religious large-group identity and how does it become intertwined with an individual's own personal identity? Answering this question will help us to appreciate Mert's struggle with his large-group identity.

Our individual identity, the uniqueness each human being experiences, is something that has evolved from childhood, an internal sense of sameness we carry with us for life, even while we share some of our characteristics with others (Erikson, 1956). On a surface level we can define ourselves using labels that identify aspects of our life, such as parent, historian, psychiatrist, musician, police officer, gardener, or basketball player. While true, these definitions do not reach the deeper sustained sameness and inner solidity that is connected with belonging to a large group beginning in childhood. Infants and small children are incapable of feeling or intellectualizing concepts of large-group identity affiliations and ideologies—ethnic, national, religious, or political. In these realms they are generalists (Erikson, 1956). The six areas outlined below can help us explore how a child stops being a "generalist" and fully embraces a large-group identity.

1. Psychobiological Potential for "We-ness"

In the previous chapter I described various scientific studies that took place in recent decades on the development of a child's mind. They revealed that a psychobiological potential for we-ness and bias toward one's own kind exists even in the early months and years of a child's life. Paul Bloom (2010) described how preferences for what we like and why, including a bias toward our own kind, begin in early childhood. But this sense of we-ness is limited because of the restricted nature of an infant's or small child's experience.

2. Separation–Individuation

In time, children begin to separate their own mental image from those of familiar Others, such as mothers and other caregivers, integrating different aspects, such as pleasant and unpleasant or libidinal and aggressive, of both types of images (Kernberg, 1976; Mahler, 1968; Mahler, Pine, & Bergman, 1975; Volkan, 1976). At twenty-four to thirty-six months, children sense "cultural amplifiers" (Mack, 1979)—concrete or abstract symbols and signs that are only associated with a specific large group. Should a nanny with a different large-group background exhibit investment in one of her own large group's cultural amplifiers, the child's mother might explain to the child that his attachment to the item isn't the same as the nanny's because his own ethnicity, nationality, or religion differ from the nanny's affiliations. Learning these differences becomes part of the child's integration of his mother's and his own images.

3. Identifications

Children identify with aspects of individuals in close relationship to them, whether these elements are realistic, fantasized, wished for, or frightening. They also embrace concrete and abstract large-group identity markers such as language, songs, mythic and historic images, religious and political beliefs, and other cultural amplifiers. Eric Erikson (1956) stated that identity formation begins where identification with the persons of the past ends. Sigmund Freud (1940a) noted that, to a child, the parents represent the general society including identification with the parents' and significant persons' prejudices, ranging from benign to hostile.

4. Depositing

In "identification" children are the primary initiators, gathering what they witness and feel from their environment and making it their own. In "depositing" it is an adult in the child's life who feels compelled to add something to the child's psyche. This is much like Melanie Klein's (1946) description of "projective identification." However, since I am describing the creation of a foundation for the child's identity formation, I prefer to use "depositing" and differentiate it from Klein's term. I have written about and given examples of depositing in my other writings (Volkan, 1988, 2013, 2014b; Volkan, Ast, & Greer, 2002). Anne Ancelin Schützenberger's "ancestor syndrome" (1998), Judith Kestenberg's "transgenerational transposition" (1982), and Haydée Faimberg's description of "the telescoping of generations" (2005), as well as many other authors' work on the intergenerational transmissions of Holocaust-related images and functions (Brenner, 2014; Kogan, 1995; Laub & Podell, 1997) refer to depositing.

When thousands or millions of children receive the same or a similar deposited item they begin to share "psychological DNA." After a collective catastrophe inflicted by an enemy group, for example, affected individuals are left with self-images similarly (though not identically) traumatized by the massive event. These many individuals deposit such images into their children and give them tasks such as: "Regain my self-esteem for me"; "Put my mourning process on the right track"; "Be assertive and take revenge"; or "Never forget and remain alert." Though each child in the second generation owns a unique individual identity, all share similar links to the same massive trauma's image and similar unconscious tasks for coping with it. If the next generation cannot effectively fulfill their shared tasks—and this is usually the case—they will pass them on to the third generation, and so on. Through the years, such conditions create an invisible but powerful network consisting of thousands or millions of people. Depositing also includes passing along various kinds of prejudicial elements concerning the unfamiliar Other.

5. Suitable Targets of Externalization

In the study of "normal" prejudice development, René Spitz's (1965) research is well known. His term "stranger anxiety" refers to the response of infants at about eight months of age, who recognize that not all the faces in their limited environment belong to their caregivers. It is their first recognition of the unfamiliar stranger, the Other. In 1988, I described "suitable targets for externalization" that *experientially* teach children, at the peak of putting their un-mended sides together, about the existence of other large groups. This process can be perceived as developing shared stranger anxiety and creating shared prejudice at the large-group level. I provided the following example.

For centuries the Greeks and Turks on Cyprus lived as neighbors, but in 1974 the island was de facto divided into two political entities. Within their close proximity, there were nevertheless "cultural amplifiers" (Mack, 1979) delineating the two groups. Muslim Turks, for example, would never eat pork, and pigs are considered unclean. Greeks on the other hand often raise pigs. Turkish and Greek children alike are drawn to animals, especially baby ones, but a Turkish child wanting to hold a piglet would be roundly discouraged by a parent or other important individuals in the Turkish child's environment. It would not be accepted by the child's large group. Taking this example further, what if the Turkish child still has some unintegrated self-images and internalized object images? Now, she finds a suitable target for her unwanted, aggressively contaminated, and unintegrated "bad" self- and object images. Since Muslim Turks do not eat pork, in a concrete sense, what is externalized into the image of the pig will not be re-internalized.

When children unconsciously find a shared suitable target for unintegrated "bad" self- and object images, such as in the example above, this precursor of the unfamiliar Other becomes established in their mind at an experimental level (Volkan, 1988, 2013, 2014a). At this point, the Turkish children in Cyprus have no idea what Greekness means. Such a sophisticated concept with associated emotions about the unfamiliar Other evolves much later, as the children incorporate perceptions and emotions around them and images of history. This happens without the children's awareness that the experientially learned symbol of the Other was in the service of helping them avoid feeling object relations tension. Since almost every Turkish child in Cyprus will use the same target, they will share the same precursor of the unfamiliar Other and invest similar prejudice in this Other.

Suitable targets also serve as reservoirs for children's libidinally loaded "good" unintegrated self- and object images. A Finnish child might use the sauna as such a reservoir for example. Sophisticated thoughts and feelings about Finnishness come later with adulthood. All cultural amplifiers—from regional food to overt national symbols such as flags—can serve as *shared* targets utilized for externalization for "good," internal images, and the unfamiliar Other's food or flag for "bad" internal images.

By utilizing these *shared* suitable targets of externalization, children experientially begin moving away from being a "generalist." Their sense of belonging to a specific large group is now more firmly established, as is their separation from the shared unfamiliar Other. This very human characteristic of belonging to a large-group identity, with its many positive aspects, is also linked to shared prejudice, which may range from benign to malignant according to history and circumstance.

6. Adolescence Passage

An individual's passage through adolescence includes an unconscious review of childhood attachments to familiar Others, and this leads to a "second individuation." Peter Blos (1962, 1967, 1979) described the crystallization of a firm sense of personal and gender identities during the passage through adolescence. Also during this time, a large-group identity that has evolved during childhood becomes a final identity (Volkan, 1997, 2004). There are circumstances that may arise during teen years and adulthood when a person may deny or repress his investment in his large-group identity of childhood. For example, an individual may have migrated to another country during later teen years or early adulthood. Even in these circumstances, however, this person's large-group identity lives on in the shadows.

There is a second category of large-group identities—those that develop in adulthood. A political party or a sports team can acquire hundreds of thousands or millions of followers; a large corporation may encompass a huge number of business leaders and employees. People identifying with such entities can be imagined as belonging in adulthood to this type of large group. However, followers of a political party or sport team or business leaders and employees do not lose their first type of large-group identity established in *childhood*. Religious cults such as Aum Shinrikyo or the Branch Davidians and terrorist organizations such as Al-Qaeda and ISIS provide good examples of such large groups. Members of terrorist organizations and lone wolves attached to them function under the dominant impact of this second type of large-group identity. They lose their individual identity's and superego's influence—such as old personal beliefs and moral attitudes—on their behavior patterns through strong utilization of a combination of defense mechanisms such as denial, repression, displacement, and intellectualization. Mass suicides sometimes occur in religious cults because members lose their superego restrictions and earlier attitudes about life. Terrorists or suicide bombers do not behave inhumanely simply because of problems their individual identities began developing in childhood. As representatives of their adulthood's large group, they perceive their horrible acts as a duty in order to protect or bring attention to their second-type large-group identity (Suistola & Volkan, 2017; Volkan, 2013).

In understanding Mert's large-group identity confusion, and his perception of himself as a "fake Turk," our focus should be on large-group identity formation in childhood. Although as a young man he was involved in leftist large-group activities for a time, it will become clear as I continue to tell his story that Mert was not under the influence of a large-group identity that establishes itself in adulthood.

CHAPTER SIX

Secrets

My aim in telling Mert's story is to illustrate the intertwining of external and internal events that shaped his psychological makeup. I will not focus much on technical issues Dr. Ufuk faced while conducting Mert's psychoanalysis or on the supervisor's suggestions and interventions. I will however explain Dr. Ufuk's and my understanding of Mert's analytic progress from a psychoanalytic point of view. In this chapter I report on what Mert talked about during the first five months on the psychoanalytic couch.

Earlier in their marriage Mert wanted his wife to assume some of the cultural Hemshin habits of his village. For example, he had demanded that his wife scrub his back and that she be involved in their son's bathing until the boy became a teenager. Soon it became clear to Mert that she had her own lifestyle agenda that would not include compliance with or fulfillment of Mert's investment in the culture in which he was raised. She declined to go to Mert's village with her husband whenever he visited his mother, father, and other relatives, and she did not appreciate her in-laws coming to Istanbul for visits. Neither did she develop a friendship with the young woman of Hemshin descent, the daughter of Mert's relative, who lived with them for a year. She had her own friends, other women who were raised in cities and who were "westernized."

Besides fears that someone would kidnap his son, his graves and ghosts phobias, and his avoiding of high places, Mert had expectations of other dangers. Every time a dog barked in the neighborhood he imagined that a thief might be entering his property, and he would grab a stick he kept on hand until all was quiet. He did not feel comfortable in his big house in Istanbul and was afraid of going into the basement lest he meet a terrorist hiding there. Mert also could not enjoy his garden because he was afraid that he might encounter a snake among his wife's flower beds. He was afraid of darkness and also had a phobia about bears. In reality, he had seen a bear only twice in his life.

Mert provided more information about his childhood. There had been no electricity in the farmhouse and the village until he was seven years old. I was not surprised to hear this. I was born in 1932 and as a child, most of the time, I lived in a middle-class Turkish section of the capital city of Cyprus, Nicosia. We did not have electricity until I was in my early teens. I recalled how I used to study at night using an oil lamp and sometimes even candles. When Mert was a child in the 1970s, Turkey was a poor country. While he attended the elementary grades, the school did not have a toilet. Instead, a hole had been dug in the schoolyard, separated from the play area by a wooden wall. Once when little Mert went there several bats flew out of the hole, causing him to be afraid of using it thereafter. Once again he recalled being beaten by a girl in the elementary school and his teacher not having any empathy for him.

More information came forth about his fear of graves. When he was a child he had seen holes someone had dug in the village cemetery. He was told that this was done in hopes of finding buried jewelry or gold, but little Mert could not comprehend fully what adults were telling him. As he grew older he learned that whenever his Hemshin ancestors were afraid of other ethnic groups coming to the village to steal, they buried their valuables. He realized that the newer generation of villagers searched for buried jewelry or gold, not in the cemetery alone, but in gardens or nearby mountains as well. Apparently, the ancestors had buried their valuable items by wrapping them in organic cyanide. Such chemical material would produce poisonous fumes that would kill or sicken any thief who was not prepared with breathing protection. This way they hoped to keep others from digging up their valuables and stealing them. As he was growing up Mert learned that some people who dug in the ground to recover jewelry or gold had actually died when the poison escaped. In a dream he saw an unknown person catching a big snake and squeezing it, producing poisonous juice that he forced into Mert's mouth. Dr. Ufuk felt that by telling the story of buried jewelry and gold her patient symbolically was expressing his hesitation to look into his historical past, even though he might have hoped to find glorified aspects of it.

Mert gave more details of his leaving the village, staying in the nearby town where he attended high school, and then going to Ankara. After arriving in Ankara for the first time by bus, he took a taxi to a place where he would stay with another young man from his village. The taxi driver deceived him by overcharging the fare, and that led him to mistrust people at his new location.

Dr. Ufuk had made an arrangement with Mert about the payment for his treatment, one that was customary for many Turkish psychoanalysts: At the end of each session the analysand leaves the money for that session on a table before leaving the analyst's office. Dr. Ufuk noted that at the end of the session during which Mert talked about not trusting the taxi drivers in Ankara, the patient had placed his money on the analyst's desk—not for just one session, but payment for three. After the patient left Dr. Ufuk realized that Mert was struggling with trusting or not trusting his analyst and unconsciously testing her. When he came to his next session Dr. Ufuk, without making a reference to Mert's story about a taxi driver cheating him, told him to make payments only for each session as they had previously agreed. She told him that he and she started to travel together on a new road, psychoanalysis, and to look around through a "new window." It would be important that during this journey he would not make the analyst owe him something by paying for sessions not already conducted. Mert never made payments for future sessions again. Since very early in his analysis, Dr. Ufuk and I sensed that Mert was also wondering about the analyst's ethnic background. Was she a "real" Turk, a Laz, or a Kurd? What did she think about a Muslim Armenian, or Armenians in general?

While in Ankara waiting to enter the university, for a long time Mert slept in the same bed with his friend. He had no money other than what his father was giving or sending him. Meanwhile, at the village his older sister had burned his high school diploma by accident, thinking of it as a piece of useless paper. The school sent a replacement to the university, and Mert was able to start attending. At the university he did not feel "entitled" to be friends with "beautiful" female students. He chose an "ugly one" with whom to be friendly. He felt unworthy to befriend a beautiful woman.

Session after session the patient spoke about traumatic events of his childhood and young years and his lack of entitlement for good things in life. One day, in the fourth month of lying on the couch, suddenly he appeared as a confident business person. He described how he was involved in a new business of building a big hotel in a Middle Eastern country. He remained excited for a week, openly showing his successful side. Then he returned to his usual characterization of himself as a "fake" person when he heard that another successful businessman who seemed to be envious of Mert's recent success referred to him as an "unimportant Armenian."

Around the same time his sister-in-law was visiting from another part of Turkey and staying in their house. Dr. Ufuk noted that Mert was "hiding" from his sister-in-law as if he was not entitled to be on her social level. One evening they arranged a dinner party. Mert reported how embarrassed he was when he could not make correct seating arrangements. He came to his session declaring that he was sick and tired. Instead of being upset with her husband for embarrassing her in front of her sister and city friends, Mert's wife wanted to purchase a big property on the outskirts of Istanbul. It was as if she wanted to be "paid" for staying married to a "fake" Turk. Without verbalizing it, Dr. Ufuk thought that she had done the right thing when she told Mert not to pay upfront for future sessions, lest she be put in a position of being bought to stay as Mert's analyst.

In the next session, Mert recalled how he learned to drive a car and then, referring to his wife and son, he exclaimed: "Love and fear together cannot remain under the same roof." He then declared he had nothing to say. Dr. Ufuk spoke at some length during this session. She linked Mert's stories of traumatic events while he was growing up, his being a "fake" university graduate and thinking of himself as a "fake Turk" to his present expectation that someone or something might humiliate him at any minute. The analyst also described her sensing how Mert was "hiding" himself on the couch. She added: "You may be wondering about my ethnicity and if I am able to understand a person of Hemshin descent. I realized that I do not yet know your wife's and son's names. There seem to be some secrets. Who says that going through analysis is an easy task? I wish we had an easier way. Today you reported how you learned to drive a car. Let us learn together how to travel without secrets."

With his next psychoanalytic session, Mert started pouring out his secrets, secrets he had not told his ten previous psychiatrists. First, he told Dr. Ufuk the names of his wife and son. His wife's name was a typical and popular Turkish name. As suggested by Mert's in-laws, the son was named after a famous Turkish historical leader. The in-laws were very nationalistic people. Here we will call him Süleyman, after Süleyman the Magnificent (1494–1566), the Sultan of the Ottoman Empire whose marble relief is one of twenty-three portraits of historical figures over the gallery doors of the House chamber in the US Capitol. Dr. Ufuk, again without verbalizing what came to her mind while she was with her analysand, thought: "No wonder my patient is afraid that someone will kidnap the boy. Having the child sleep in the parental bedroom—among other reasons—was to keep Turkishness, represented by his son, in the room and then hide the father's Hemshin descent."

Mert's wife had told her own mother about Süleyman sleeping in the parental bedroom and her husband's refusal to send the boy to sleep in another room. The mother knew that her daughter had, for all practical purposes, no sex life. She had been telling her daughter to divorce Mert. But, instead of leaving her husband, she was asking for favors to increase her self-esteem. Dr. Ufuk learned that Mert had bought three houses for his wife that she rented out. Now she was asking to be the owner of another, bigger property. At home, Mert's wife never cooked or did hard work. She would never wear a fancy dress more than once. Using her husband's money, she was having, or pretending to have, a high social life, most of the time without her husband accompanying her.

Mert reported another dream, in which his wife wanted him to buy a ticket for her to attend a fancy social event. In the dream, Mert bought ten tickets instead of one. Telling this dream Mert became more aware of his paying his wife to remain married to a *Hemşinli* man. Thereafter, Mert began to bring dreams to his sessions regularly. Instead of one dream, he would bring several, at one time ten dreams, and tell them one after another as if he was reading a newspaper. I suggested that Dr. Ufuk not pay much attention to the contents of these dreams and instead to wonder why her patient was flooding her with dreams, even giving her ten dreams like he had purchased ten tickets for his wife. She told her patient that he was also giving her gifts by presenting many dreams in each session. She did not need to have such "gifts." It would be better for the two of them to observe together what might be hiding behind such gifts. There was no reason for him to be a "fake" analysand.

Mert brought up his biggest secret, his having another woman in his life. Five years prior to his marriage, he had met a widow. This woman was six years older than the patient and had a daughter who was now in her early twenties. She did not belong to the high society of Istanbul. The patient made arrangements to visit this widow two times a week and have sex with her. The patient did not have erectile dysfunction with this older woman. Mert continued with this arrangement after he was married and financially helped the widow to have a comfortable life. Mert's wife had no idea about his affair. Mert had confessed the affair to his mother, who referred to this woman as a "prostitute." Mert became very disappointed. His mother told him: "You see, if you were married to a woman of our kind, someone from our village, you would not have these problems." Dr. Ufuk wondered if the older woman represented a mother figure for her patient and if the relationship with her had something to do with Mert's oedipal issues. If this was so, she could understand Mert's disappointment when his mother called his lover a "prostitute." Mert's mother did not tell her son to stop his affair. Dr. Ufuk and I thought that it would induce anxiety and resistance to the analytic work if the analyst turned Mert's attention to oedipal issues at this time; so instead, she decided to wait and let Mert feel freer to express himself.

Mert confessed that the widow had become pregnant by him before he was married to his wife. At that time the widow wanted Mert to marry her but he encouraged her to have an abortion and she went along with this. Afterwards Mert felt terrible. "I thought I was having a psychotic break" he declared. The widow continued her efforts to marry Mert, but he continued to refuse and then married someone else. However, the widow continued to satisfy Mert sexually; in a sense, as Dr. Ufuk thought, the widow was also "bought" by Mert and hidden from other people except Mert's mother. The analyst now could hear that this widow was more than the representation of a mother figure. She also might represent the analysand's humiliated self, his "hidden" belongingness to the Hemshin people. Mert could be a man with an erect penis at the widow's house since the humiliated self was externalized onto the woman. On the other hand, at his own home he was a *Hemşinli* while his wife's people were the "real" Turks.

In his own house Mert could not even masturbate freely. He had to hide somewhere in his house whenever he had an urge to do so. Meanwhile, his wife's family had to be satisfied while he seemed obliged to respond to their needs. It turned out that his wife's father was only a high school graduate, and Mert's "high-society wife" was trying to repress this fact. The father-in-law had stopped working as soon as his daughter married Mert. Whenever the in-laws visited Mert and his family, Mert felt uncomfortable sitting down and having dinner with them. One reason for this was his father-in-law's ultra-nationalistic boasting and talk about the extreme right-wing political organization to which he belonged. This man would even say something like, "We smashed the Armenian people." His son-in-law had studied the history of the Hemshin people and knew he was of Armenian descent, but his father-in-law believed that the Hemshin people were originally from Scotland and had come to Crimea centuries ago, later becoming Muslims and Turks. After all, Mert and some Hemshin people had blond hair and blue eyes like Scottish people. The older man felt completely free to speak against Armenians in front of his son-in-law.

The husband of one of Mert's wife's sisters was working as a junior partner at Mert's factory. Dr. Ufuk learned that this man was mixed up with a Turkish mafia. When Mert had sent this man to a Middle Eastern country for a building project, the man stole Mert's money to pay what he owed the mafia. Because he and Mert's sister-in-law still had some debt when he returned to Istanbul, they went into hiding. Mert's connection with this man appeared to provide a realistic reason for Mert's fear of someone kidnapping Süleyman. He was afraid that the mafia might find a way to read his emails in order to find where his wife's relatives were hiding. The first time on the couch he expressed anger about his wife's family using his money to take care their own family problems. He recounted a dream about a long tunnel through which he travelled with his wife. At the end of the tunnel someone cut his wife's head off. But soon her head was put back into place. After reporting this dream Mert said: "If my head was cut off, no one would put it back!"

I was pleased with Dr. Ufuk's ability to listen to her analysand's secrets. It was now clear that Mert was exhibiting issues above and beyond the problems of a typical neurotic individual that needed to be understood and analyzed. Dr. Ufuk most likely would not have started analyzing Mert as her second analytic case if she or I or her psychoanalytic institute's committee that approves a candidate's cases for suitability for analysis had known or guessed how complicated Mert's case would become. We can say that psychoanalysts have no experience in the lifestyle of mafia members outside of what they may watch in movies and on television. At that time several Turkish television series, such as the popular *Behzat Ç* and *Kaçak*, were based on Turkish mafia stories, but I learned that Dr. Ufuk did not have a habit of watching television shows. Mert's remarks about the mafia's capacity for revenge are not things that psychoanalysts routinely hear from their patients. One of my patients in the United States was the grandson of an Italian mafia leader. The young man, the favorite grandson, in fact had started his analysis after his grandfather was brutally murdered in front of his house (Volkan, 1976). My knowledge about how a mafia family functioned in the United States came in handy to understand Mert's concerns about a Turkish mafia.

More secrets came out about Mert's background. They were also linked to his phobias about dangerous things, which had started in his childhood. His adult experiences due to political and historical events would be condensed with his childhood experiences and his separation–individuation and oedipal issues. His symptoms and behavior patterns would also be used to deal with additional pressures. While Mert was a university student the political protests and violence in Turkey related to the clash between right-wing ultra-nationalists and left-wing opposition sometimes reemerged. Mert belonged to a far-left group. He was excited and also afraid when he was asked to build a Molotov cocktail, a bottle bomb, to set a target ablaze. In the end he was relieved from performing this task. One day the police came to the place where his group was gathering. According to Mert, the police planted weapons in this location and then claimed that these weapons belonged to the leftist student group. Mert and his friends were taken to prison and Mert was beaten badly by the police. He was lucky because he was allowed to leave the prison after ten days when no proof of his involvement in a criminal act was found. One of his friends who was also taken to prison was Kurdish. Later this man would become a member of PKK. Meanwhile, after graduating from the university, Mert did his compulsory military service for a year without any trouble. The rest of his life, even after he became a successful businessman, the patient worried about someone learning of his involvement in the leftist student group, his having the task of making a Molotov cocktail, and being a friend of a Kurdish person who later was considered a PKK terrorist and a killer. Dr. Ufuk wondered if Mert felt that he was also a murderer when he urged the widow to have an abortion. At this time Mert made no connection to the aborted fetus, so his analyst kept what had come to her mind to herself, thinking that this issue might come up later and be discussed then. Mert was extremely careful about being very honest and open in his business affairs. But someone who might know his past would see him potentially as a dangerous person, a former friend of a Kurdish terrorist. Here too his being perceived as a "fake Turk" had to be covered up.

CHAPTER SEVEN

Canyon of Hell

During the second part of his first year in analysis Mert began to talk more and more about his extended family and his ancestors. I suggested to Dr. Ufuk not to interfere and let him express himself. I felt that for Mert not to feel like a "fake" Turk he needed to explore the contamination of his personal identity with his ancestors' history and accept what he wanted to keep within himself and what to discard for improving his self-esteem. Then he could be in a position to allow himself to resolve pathological influences of the usual childhood psychosexual and aggressive fantasies and be a "real" man.

We learned more about Mert's family of Hemshin descent. At this time his father was seventy-three and his mother was sixty-three years old. When Mert was a child his mother did not know more than 100 Turkish words, but by at least a decade prior to Mert coming to see Dr. Ufuk, almost everyone in the region where he was born had learned Turkish. Both of his parents belonged to the same extended family unit. They had become engaged when Mert's mother was only thirteen years old and were soon married. Mert's paternal grandfather had died due to an accident: he fell from a tree into a river and hit his head on a stone. At that time Mert's father was twelve years old. Since his two older brothers had died earlier due to some illness, he became the man of the family at a young age. When Mert was born his father was twenty-five and his mother, who already had a daughter, was nineteen years old. Mert told his analyst that his mother had gone to the toilet where she ended up giving birth to him. He seemed to be embarrassed that he had been born in a toilet. On the couch he realized that he did not have "good enough parents" (Winnicott, 1965). Many relatives, including his paternal grandmother, would look after the children on and off. As an adult he became rich in order to "buy" some "good enough things," but still felt that he was not entitled to have them. He had "bought" a beautiful wife, but he could not make love to her. He had a huge house, but he could not even feel free to enter its basement. He was both a "fake" Turk and a "fake" rich man, doomed to search for entitlement for "good enough" things.

Mert recalled killing a puppy by choking it when he was a child. This most likely reflected his experiencing rage about something, but he could not recall any details linked to this event. Instead he began talking about scary aggressive stories he used to hear when he was growing up. There were honor killings. If a family felt that the family honor was injured they would kill a member or members of the perpetrator family. When Mert was six years old, one of his uncles on his father's side was murdered. Mert's father, the head of the extended family, could not prevent the death of his own brother. After this event Mert's father turned to religion; he never drank alcohol. However, since he did not have a close relationship with his son, Mert grew up without much investment in religion. He did not identify with the defensive religious aspects of the father's behavior. There was, however, identification with a different aspect of his father. As a child, Mert realized that his father had phobias about graves. He had followed his father in having an identical symptom.

When Mert was growing up he would hear stories of a graveyard that no longer existed, and as an adult he had an urge to collect information about this missing graveyard. He was not sure about the accuracy of what he learned, but he believed that this missing graveyard was the burial place for Hemshin people when they were Christians. He found out that Christian Hemshin people had settled in the area starting around the year 1700. Then 1,000 or 2,000 of them became Muslims. Others escaped or were killed and also buried in the Christian cemetery. Later this cemetery was destroyed, perhaps by the Muslim Hemshin people.

There were also stories of Muslim Hemshin people's fights with other ethnic groups living nearby, especially Laz people. As a child Mert knew of a place the Hemshin people called the *Canyon of Hell*. He had heard that one time Laz people attacked Hemshin people, driving thousands of them to the edge of a mountain and forcing them to fall to their death in the canyon below.

Mert learned that there was a series of wars between the Ottomans and Russians from 1568 to World War I. During the Russo-Turkish War from 1768 to 1774 the Russian military entered the Caucasus. In 1828 Russians conquered Armenia and reached the Ottoman border. This created various deadly events between Armenians and people in the Ottoman territory next to the Ottoman–Armenian border. When Ottomans fought the Russians during World War I Armenians entered the eastern part of the Ottoman Empire. Without focusing on the details of Armenia's history and without examining in depth what was true and what were fantasized or mythologized shared perceptions, Mert began talking about how Christian Armenians from Armenia had come to Turkey and killed Muslim Hemshin people, even though the latter were also of Armenian descent. Mert thought that Muslim Hemshin people may have begun burying their jewelry and gold at this time. He did not mention what Ottoman Turks, in turn, did to Armenians within the Ottoman Empire in 1915. His focus was on how his childhood mind was filled with danger, dead people, and ghosts. He was not truly a part of the Christian Armenians; yet, he was not truly a Muslim "Turk."

CHAPTER EIGHT

The Supervisor's Thoughts and Feelings

In the psychoanalytic literature we can find material dealing with senior analysts' supervisory work with psychoanalytic candidates in training. There has been no focus on what kinds of thoughts and feelings are induced in a senior analyst's mind when he or she hears the supervised analyst's patient's story. In this chapter I will describe what kinds of personal memories and emotions came to my mind while listening to Mert's struggle with his large-group identity. As the reader will notice my memories and emotions are also linked to large-group identity relationships.

One year after my arriving in the United States in early 1957 I began my psychiatric residency training at the Memorial Hospital of the University of North Carolina in Chapel Hill. The psychoanalytic approach was the dominant approach in our training. I also noted how psychoanalysis was popular among scholars who were studying human history and human expression when I realized that many individuals from the Department of History and the Department of English were undergoing psychoanalysis with some of my mentors. During the 1957 Christmas address at the American Historical Association, William Langer, then president of this association, declared that the next assignment for historians should be paying attention to depth psychology. After finishing my psychiatric training, I moved to Charlottesville, Virginia and started my academic career at the Medical School of the University of Virginia. I also began traveling from

Charlottesville to Washington, DC where I underwent my own training psychoanalysis and where I attended the Washington Psychoanalytic Institute and then became a psychoanalyst myself. When I was undergoing my psychoanalysis, deadly ethnic troubles were taking place in my birthplace Cyprus between Cypriot Greeks and Cypriot Turks. During the last two of my medical school years in Ankara I shared a room with another Cypriot Turk who was about two years younger than me and who was also attending my medical school. I had no male sibling and he had become like my brother. A few months after I arrived in the United States he went to Cyprus from Ankara to visit his ailing mother. When he went to a pharmacy to purchase medicine for her, he was killed by a Cypriot Greek terrorist who shot him seven times. Looking back, I realize that my analyst, and in turn I, did not focus on the deadly historical events my family members and my friends in Cyprus were going through. Analysts in the United States whose works I was following at that time were not like William Langer. They were not saying that the next assignment for psychoanalysts should be paying attention to shared history. Only decades later I realized that my writing a book on what happened in Cyprus (1979) and another book on mourning (1981) early in my academic career were in the service of my working through the impact that external events in Cyprus had on me and my complicated mourning of losing my roommate while I was living safely in America. I think that unconsciously, through my writing, I had found a way to take care of issues that were not taken care of while I was on my analyst's couch.

On 19 November 1977 Egyptian President Anwar Sadat went to Israel and at the Knesset declared that there was a psychological wall between Arabs and Israelis and that this barrier was constituting 70 percent of problems between these large groups. The American Psychiatric Association's Committee on Psychiatry and Foreign Affairs started bringing together high-level Israelis and Egyptians to see if Sadat's remarks were correct. I had just become a member of this Committee and would become its chairperson three years later. Our task of bringing together Israelis and Egyptians, also later Palestinians, lasted more than five years. Then, in 1987, I founded the Center for the Study of Mind and Human Interaction (CSMHI) at the University of Virginia's Medical School with a multidisciplinary team. Until CSMHI was closed in 2005, its interdisciplinary team worked with Americans and Soviets, Russians and Estonians, Georgians and South Ossetians, Croats and Serbians, Turks and Greeks, and others. We spent time in places such as Albania following the death of dictator Enver Hoxha, and Kuwait after Saddam Hussein's forces were pushed out, and also visited refugee camps. I continued to be involved in international relations after CSMHI no longer existed (Volkan, 1988, 1997, 2004, 2006, 2013, 2014a). I realized that in order to understand the psychological sentiments shared by thousands or millions of people within a national, ethnic, religious, or politically ideological large group our team required the help of a historian. I worked closely with historian Norman Itzkowitz from Princeton University and also, for a shorter time, historian and psychoanalyst Peter Loewenberg from the University of California. My work in international affairs led me to note and pay attention to historical and political events in the clinical setting too; some patients need to talk about such events while undergoing psychoanalysis.

Listening to Dr. Ufuk and hearing about Mert's focus on the Armenian–Turkish conflicts induced certain feelings in me. As Dr. Ufuk's supervisor, I kept these feelings to myself and did not share them with her. I recalled that when I was growing up in Cyprus, Christian Armenians in Nicosia lived within the areas where Turkish Cypriots lived or in places between the Turkish and Greek neighborhoods. All of them also spoke Turkish. As a child I felt that Armenians with another large-group identity were much closer to my people than the Greeks were. When I was in my late teens we moved to my maternal grandfather's big house after his death, and our next-door neighbors were Armenians. Every week from my latency and through my early teen years I, and also my two sisters, would go to Armenian Vahan Bedelyan's house for our violin lessons. It was he who introduced me to Mozart, Beethoven, Paganini, and others from the Western music world. My violin teacher and I would converse in Turkish. I recall going to the Armenian church not far from my grandfather's house as a prepubescent boy to practice and play violin with Vahan Bedelyan's other students and performing for the first time in front of an audience. I vividly remember my first visit there, seeing many priests who were only speaking Armenian and wearing robes belted with knotted rope. As a child I had been exposed to a widely held myth that each knot represented a child strangled by the wearer. Since I was not a Christian, I felt I might be a target of their aggression. It took me a few visits before I could enjoy the musical aura of this church. Bedelyan, a famous violinist, was a well-known and loved person within the Cypriot Turkish community. He also taught music at my Turkish high school in Nicosia after my graduation, and my older sister, also a teacher, was his assistant. Two years ago, when I was visiting the island, I was not surprised to learn that some art lovers within the Cypriot Turkish community in Nicosia still remember Bedelyan and honor his memory.

There are an estimated 3,500 Armenians living in Cyprus, mostly in Nicosia. They have a long history there. Recently I learned that Vahan Bedelyan's family had come to Cyprus when it was under the British rule from Konya, a city in the middle of Anatolia. I wondered if he, a Christian Armenian, had left Anatolia for a British colony to be in a safer location. When deadly ethnic troubles were going on between Cypriot Greeks and Cypriot Turks in 1963, Armenians left their houses that were located within the Turkish communities and moved to the Greek areas. I suspect that they felt safer by doing this. Also recently I learned that during these difficult times two Armenians were killed by some extremist Cypriot Turks with the idea that Christian Armenians might take the Christian Greeks' side. At the present time all Cypriot Armenians live on the Greek side of the island. The Armenian churches and some Armenian houses still remain empty on the Turkish side.

In July 2018 Cypriot Turkish artists, with the collaboration of artists from the Greek side of the island, France, and the United Kingdom organized an exhibition in an empty and rundown but still beautiful Armenian house in front of the newly renovated Armenian church where I played my violin as a child. Since I was visiting Cyprus I had the opportunity to attend the opening of this exhibition. These artists have created their works of art through their own personal interpretation and understanding of this building. My niece, well-known artist Nilgün Güney, hung a picture of Vahan Bedelyan playing his violin on a wall next to my sisters' and my childhood pictures. For me they were perfect symbols characterizing the friendly togetherness of the past between Armenians and Turks living on the island.

When I was in medical school in Turkey I do not recall anyone saying negative things about the Armenians. My uncle was the chairperson of the Department of Ophthalmology, and one of his assistants who was our teacher was a Christian Armenian, a Turkish citizen. I recall how close I felt toward him because, like me, he spoke Turkish with an accent—his was Armenian and mine Cypriot Turkish.

It was after I came to the United States that I was exposed to the horrible history of what had happened to Armenians in 1915 in the Ottoman Empire, their murder and deportation to new locations. My ignorance of these most tragic events when I was in medical school in Turkey might be due to the following factor: Murdering and deporting Armenians took place during the very last period of the Ottoman Empire, and Turks living in the new Turkey whom I knew during the 1950s were also distancing themselves from that period. In a sense we erased the people who were in power during the last period of the Ottoman Empire from our minds. Our thoughts were filled with excitement about modernization and westernization of the new Turkish identity.

Soon after I became a psychiatrist in the United States, in the mid-1960s, I attended an American Psychiatric Association annual meeting in Honolulu. One evening at dinner I was sitting with thirty or forty psychiatrists around a long table. The psychiatrist sitting next to me noted that I was speaking English with an accent. He asked me about my background. I answered: "I am Turkish." He literally started shaking with fear. I learned that he was an Armenian-American and that sitting next to a Turk was a most fearful and unacceptable thing for him. I was shocked.

In 2001, initiated by the Americans, perhaps the Department of State, the Turkish Armenian Reconciliation Commission (TARC) was established. It would bring together influential Turks and influential Armenians—including former high-level Turkish and Armenian diplomats, such as a former foreign minister from Turkey—for dialogues on the Turkish–Armenian relationship. The Armenian team had Armenian-American members. I was asked to join the Turkish team even though I was not a Turkish citizen and had never been one. I have described my observations of TARC in some detail elsewhere (Volkan, 2006). I recall how an Armenian commissioner opened the first meeting I attended. He said: "During the last many decades we were able to raise a huge amount of money and with it we plan to build a huge monument in Washington, DC for the Armenian genocide at the hands of the Turks in 1915. If you Turks accept that there was an Armenian genocide and apologize for it, our monument will show the Turks in a better light. If you do not accept that there was an Armenian genocide, the proposed memorial will make the Turks appear really horrible people. You have a choice to make!" (Volkan, 2006, p. 149). The American facilitator's methodology, turning the meetings into bargaining sessions, made any progress impossible. I had experience in bringing together representatives of opposing large groups through my Center for the Study of Mind and Human Interaction (CSMHI) team. We would help the participants get to know one another as fellow human beings. There was no room for anything similar at

TARC gatherings, however. As the reader can imagine the "historical truth" of the massive tragedy in 1915 was presented differently by members of both parties who seemed to have information about what had happened. Since I had no expertise in 1915 events I only listened. The Turks' reference to how Armenians were leaving out information about the massive Armenian rebellion against the Turks as an aspect of events under review fell on deaf Armenian ears. During the second year of the TARC meetings the Turkish team proposed the formation of a group of well-known historians from different countries who would be accepted as "neutral" by both the Turks and the Armenians. These historians would come to Istanbul to examine all documents pertaining to 1915, which would be made available to them by the Turkish government. Also, TARC members, both the Armenians and the Turks, would be present to observe and follow closely these historians' work. On the Turkish side there was no denial of massive tragedies. The expected result would be the neutral historians' conclusion as to whether or not these tragedies could be called a genocide. The Armenians refused this proposal. Instead, during the last part of the second year of TARC's existence, they agreed with the Americans in charge of TARC to hire an American law firm to decide whether or not the 1915 events were legally considered "genocide." This law firm never got in touch with the Turkish commissioners or, as far as I know, with any Turkish authority. The Turkish members were surprised when representatives of this law firm suddenly appeared at a TARC meeting and declared that legally speaking, genocide was committed. However, since a long time had passed since 1915, Turkey would not have any legal obligation to satisfy the Armenians' demand for compensation from Turkey. I suspected that the law firm was presenting the American "solution" for the Armenian–Turkish problem. As the reader can guess, both Turkish and Armenian commissioners found the law firm's conclusion unacceptable. The result was a mess. I felt sad that the way the TARC meetings were conducted made a positive outcome impossible. I became the first Turkish commissioner to resign from the Turkish team because I had become convinced that TARC meetings would go nowhere. Some other Turkish members also resigned, but TARC meetings continued. I have no information about what happened during the following TARC meetings which ended in early 2014. What I described above is not available in present-day electronic media concerning TARC.

What I want to say here is that I observed that the members of the Turkish team genuinely wished to understand the Armenian members' feelings and show empathy. When empathy was shown, however, it would complicate the discussions, since it would disturb the Armenians' large-group identity of which a major marker included the image of "bad Turks." Once we met in Istanbul. When we invited Christian Armenians who were Turkish citizens living in Istanbul to join one of our social events, the local Armenians expressed their disappointment towards the Armenian commissioners for their modeling the Armenian massive tragedy after the Holocaust. I learned that hundreds of emails and telephone messages were forwarded from Armenia and the Armenian diaspora to the Armenian commissioners not to weaken their positions. No such phenomenon occurred on the Turkish side against the Armenian commissioners or Armenians in general. I recall imagining the feelings and identity issues of Armenians who were Turkish citizens. When I began hearing Mert's story I kept wondering about the feelings of Hemshin people, beyond Mert's own situation. Now I know that "Muslim Armenians" are also degraded by real Armenians. During his analysis, Mert made no reference to the 1915 horrors. And, during the TARC meetings there was no mention of the Hemshin people.

My participation in TARC meetings also made me aware of an aspect of the societal situation in Turkey on an emotional level. During one TARC gathering we realized that all Turkish commissioners from Turkey, except one whose ancestors had always lived in Anatolia, were children of Turks forced from their homes by the former Christian subjects of the Ottoman Empire. An estimated five million Turkish and other Muslims were forcibly displaced from their homes, after repeated wars in the Balkans and the Caucasus, to migrate to the heartland of Turkey, Anatolia, by former non-Muslim subjects of the empire, aided by Christian Europeans and Russians. Turks also had escaped from Arab lands when the Europeans colonized these areas. According to estimates, another five million were killed (McCarthy, 1995). "European propaganda enhanced the idea that Ottomans were just giving back the territories they had held for centuries to their rightful owners, creating a 'moral' background and justification for 'forgetting' five million who were exiled and another five million who were killed" (Volkan, 2006, p. 152). At the homes of the Turkish commissioners whose ancestors were displaced from their original locations, mourning had been denied; their ancestors did not complain about their forced exile. This was very different than what they were hearing from the Armenian commission-ers about the Armenian homes where wounds were kept open and shared with children from their childhood on. When I started supervising younger psychoanalysts' cases in Turkey I started hearing stories of several patients whose ancestors had come from Bulgaria, Yugoslavia, or Abkhazia. Large-group identity issues had a big impact on their internal worlds.

I realized something else. When the new Turkey was born, Kemal Atatürk and his friends, in a sense, approached it as if it were, in Peter Loewenberg's (1995) term, a "synthetic nation," where people come voluntarily from different places with different cultural experiences to create a synthesis of disparate influences and live together under the huge umbrella of a new large-group identity. Loewenberg speaks of the United States and Israel as examples of synthetic nations. We must, however, remember that the African slaves did not come to the US voluntarily, and many Arabs living in Israel will not wish to be a part of a synthesis.

People whose ancestors came from different places long ago or during the last decades of the Ottoman Empire to the area of the present Turkish republic with different ethnic and religious sentiments were put under the new Turkish identity, and attempts were made to treat them equally. Loewenberg writes that synthetic nations need a mythic common past, usually glorious and sometimes persecuting, and develop self-worshipping in order to firm up the synthesis. The mythic past that was introduced in Turkey, however, was made up of glorified stories of Turkishness that had taken place in central Asia before the Turks had come to Anatolia. The creation of the new Turkey in this way has been, generally speaking, successful. However, glorified stories of Turkishness were not fully assimilated by many individuals in Anatolia who had different ethnic backgrounds. While Mert was in analysis, political attempts to change the Turkish identity once more by making it more religious and returning it to old Ottoman customs, such as—among other things—building hundreds and hundreds of new mosques or women covering their heads, have created severe ethnic, religious, and ideological fragmentations within Turkey.

I learned that Özcan Alper, a well-known moviemaker in Turkey, is of Hemshin descent and that he had made a film, *Momi*, showing the life of Hemshin people in Turkey. *Momi* was released in 2000, and I was able to watch this short film (https://www.youtube.com/watch?v=BT5rK4qHmuU). The film describes the everyday activity of a boy, other children, and adults on a huge field, empty except for the presence of some horses and village houses. Watching the film gave me a better sense of Mert's childhood. Apparently Özcan Alper was accused of harming the unity of the state by making this movie in which everyone speaks their original language. Turkish translation is provided. Also, I learned that he did not go to trial. Mert never mentioned this movie. As I stated earlier, a television series called *Kaçak* was popular. The main charter is a policeman who had killed a mobster's son. In order to protect himself from the mobster's revenge he changes his identity and goes to a new town to have a comfortable life. But, new events make his life complicated again. In Turkish "*kaçak*" means "fugitive." Several times I heard that Mert called himself "*kaçak*," a person who left his *Hemşinli* environment and moved to Istanbul. Sometimes he would say, "I want to love myself, but not as a *kaçak*." Mert described feeling guilty because, without financial help from his father, he would not have been able to start his factory and become a rich man in the city, away from his birthplace. He had given jobs at his factory and hotel to relatives and other people from the village who had come to Istanbul. But, he also felt that he had left his mother and father behind, not only because of the physical distance from them but because he was married to a woman from a family who looked down on his village relatives and who pretended to belong to high society.

When I heard of Mert's father-in-law's remarks about "smashing Armenian people" and one businessman calling Mert an "unimportant Armenian," I felt uncomfortable and sad. I thought about the difficulties Mert could face in becoming a psychologically independent man in today's political environment in Turkey. Without telling her, I paid more attention to Dr. Ufuk's own responses to the fragmentation in Turkey to which sometimes she would refer with anxiety. Once more, I was pleased at how she was developing a strong psychoanalytic identity, and Mert's being a *Hemşinli* was not at all challenging her therapeutic approach.

CHAPTER NINE

Having an "Analytic Object"

For many months while Mert was pouring out information about himself and sharing data that he had kept secret, he would sometimes miss his sessions because of his need to travel for work. He would not give much information about his business, and his analyst sensed that Mert seemed uninterested in presenting his successful business side. He needed her to hear the tension within his psyche.

After being on the analyst's couch about nine months, Mert recalled how at the beginning of his analysis he had once paid for sessions that had not taken place. He recalled how he was impressed when Dr. Ufuk told him that it would not be proper for him to do so; she did not wish to be in a position in which she would owe him something; she did not wish to be bought. He stated that recently he found himself thinking and feeling that his analyst was different than those in his life whom he "could buy." "I feel freer to open up and tell you everything. I cannot do this with my wife." He added: "Yesterday I told my wife that I come to see you four times a week and that I do not see you only once week. I am not in psychotherapy. I am in analysis."

Mert ended by confessing that after he started his analysis he kept thinking of going through another type of treatment without informing his analyst. He had heard of a therapist, also a woman, who was an expert in curing people's symptoms by hypnosis. He visited her once to hear what she could offer him. Many times he wanted and was almost attempted to be a patient of this hypnotist too. He now began realizing that there were dual aspects of himself and also that searching for two objects responding to these aspects had been part of his existence: He was a "Turk," and an "Armenian Muslim;" he was a successful man and he was someone with a long list of phobias; he had a wife and a mistress; he lived in a city but most of the time in his dreams he was in his village. He had Dr. Ufuk to help him but also wished to be treated by a hypnotist. Positive and trusting feelings he had developed about Dr. Ufuk, however, prevented him from being involved secretly with another "therapist."

Mert was describing his perception of Dr. Ufuk as an "analytic object" (sometimes called "new object," or "developmental object") (Cameron, 1961; Giovacchini, 1972; Kernberg, 1975; Loewald, 1960; Tähkä, 1993; Volkan, 1976, 2010). An analysand's interaction with an analytic object is akin to a nurturing child–mother relationship (Ekstein, 1966; Rapaport, 1951). Individuals with structural deficits or developmental arrests need to experience the analyst as an analytic object and identify with it in order to make structural changes within themselves, integrate their self-representation and external and internalized object images, and move up on the developmental ladder. Now Mert was verbalizing his crystallization of Dr. Ufuk as an analytic object in his mind and his sensing his own psychological development.

Mert went back to earlier times when he was suspicious about his analyst's investment in someone of Hemshin descent. Now we realized that beneath this transference expectation he was also developing basic trust in his analyst. Listening to her patient, Dr. Ufuk remembered one of Mert's dreams he had told her some months before. In the dream Mert was coming to Istanbul for the first time in his life. He could not find his way around, and he could not find a hotel because he was speaking a language that no one could understand. Dr. Ufuk recalled how after hearing Mert's dream she had said to him: "In this room we speak the same language. I understand you." It was after this exchange between them that Mert talked about his biggest secret, his years-long affair with the widow.

Toward the end of the first year of his analysis Mert confessed that he used his computer to find out who Dr. Ufuk was. In the old days, before the internet and other communication technologies, analysts could easily protect their personal identity and personal investments from their analysands. I was pleased to hear that Dr. Ufuk had been careful never to share detailed information about her personal life online. Mert was able to see the location in Turkey where Dr. Ufuk was born. That city, where she had spent the first years of her life, has a large Kurdish population. Mert reported how he had fantasized that Dr. Ufuk was a Kurdish person. He hinted how in his mind he linked his analyst with his friend who had become a member of PKK, but Dr. Ufuk continued to refrain from telling Mert anything personal about herself. Once more she reminded him of his dream in which he saw himself coming to Istanbul for the first time and not being understood because of his language. She told the patient once more that she and Mert were speaking the same language in her office. She added, "Learn about me in this room."

Following this session Mert was able to recall aspects of his childhood in more detail. For example, seeing his grandmother urinating and the first time he noticed what a woman's genital area looked like. He recalled how some Hemshin people referred to the Canyon of Hell as *Sesli Kaya* (Rock with a Voice). The patient could easily see how his phobia of graves and ghosts was linked to his childhood fantasy of being pushed into the Canyon of Hell, hearing screams, and his identification with his father's symptom.

CHAPTER TEN

"Second Look" Experiences

Mert came to one of his sessions early and walked around the neighborhood where his analyst's office is located, implying that this activity represented his wish to get to know her in a more realistic fashion. He informed Dr. Ufuk that he had taken his wife and son by car to various areas of Istanbul that he had never visited before. He declared: "I want to learn how to become a social person." Around this time, in one of his sessions, he declared that his Turkish was not good enough. Dr. Ufuk had never noticed her analysand having such a problem. While talking, Mert uttered three words in the language of his childhood instead of using Turkish words, as if he did not know the Turkish versions of these words. Noticing this, he translated these words into Turkish. The three words he used in Armenian stood for an "alarm bell," "making a mistake," and "blood." During a supervision hour, Dr. Ufuk and I wondered about the possible meanings and functions of Mert's uttering these words. At one level, we imagined these words were summarizing his anxiety, his being a "fake" person and his fear of danger. We also recalled how recently he was speaking about his investment in two things at the same time when describing his existence and referring to his emotional investments. Was his combining Turkish and Armenian in words also an attempt to integrate the division within him? We chose to wait.

Mert began to illustrate what Samuel Novey (1968) described as "second look" experiences. Such experiences refer to how some analysands go to their childhood locations and/or talk with adults who were around during their childhood after they gain understanding of or begin to work through some internal problems. During such visits or talks the analysands seek realistic information to verify their newly gained insights. This helps them to give up some of their symptoms.

Mert reported how he called his mother, told her about undergoing psychoanalysis, and asked her to tell him about the life on the farm and the village as she had experienced it. His mother told him how, when she was a child, she would hear stories of very difficult times in this region of Turkey. She was told that some eighty years before she was born there was famine in this area alongside ethnic difficulties. During her childhood cultural customs were tough on children. Children were not supposed to talk spontaneously when they were present in a gathering of adults. She also said that when Mert was born he was swaddled for many months.

Hearing this last piece of information did not surprise me. Most likely I was swaddled as a baby; it was a cultural custom to swaddle babies for six to nine months. When Orhan Öztürk and I (Öztürk & Volkan, 1971) studied the child-rearing practices in Turkey we were aware that swaddling does not impede motor development to any significant degree, but we knew little about its psychological effects. We wrote that:

> Any possible effects of swaddling can be evaluated in terms of the general attitudes of the parents during and after the swaddling period. It is possible that swaddling of newborns offers initially a womblike protective device in certain physical and societal conditions, but a parental swaddling tendency may be persisting beyond infancy, and therefore, it would be rather difficult to evaluate whether the assumed effects are due to the close wrapping or the swaddling tendencies of the parents (p. 218).

Mert's mother talked about her son's passivity in his early childhood. But, Dr. Ufuk and I could not find a definite link between Mert's narrowing his world as a small child and his being swaddled as a baby. Our earlier description of his not having "good enough" parents made more sense to explain his passivity. His mother apparently was aware of this. She told her son how she urged him when he was a child to cut off a chicken's head in order to teach him to be manly. Usually in a village, men cut the head off chickens, and then women pull out the feathers and cook the chicken for a meal. Mert wondered if his parents also slept in the same area where he slept with his siblings. His mother confirmed this. She told him how a mouse bit one of his toes when he was still a baby.

Some external events initiated other very active second look activities in Mert. The analyst took a two-week vacation for the first time. Without being conscious of it, Dr. Ufuk was away from her patient on the 100th Anniversary of Armenian Genocide Memorial Day, on 23 April. On this day Mert spent hours on Google reading about what Armenians and Westerners were saying about the Armenian genocide. He also read how Turks were accusing the Armenians of distorting history in a systematic fashion. His computer research was interrupted when his mother called and informed him of the unexpected death of one of his cousins. This cousin was seventy years old and very healthy. While opening the door of his car a truck had hit him. He did not die immediately; he kept screaming until he died. Mert told his mother that he would come for the funeral, and he flew to a city near his village and rented a car.

He had gained insights about his phobias concerning graves during his analysis. He kept watching himself to see if he could sense a change when the time came for him to drive through a cemetery. He was very pleased that this time he had no anxiety. That evening he told his mother about his phobias and his understanding of events in his life and the influence of his ancestors' history in their appearance. He did not tell her that now he was also trying to learn about recent Armenian history and what had happened to Christian Armenians as the Ottoman Empire was collapsing. While talking to his mother Dr. Ufuk kept coming to his mind. He realized it was as if he were an analyst himself explaining causes of a symptom to his mother. He was aware of his identification with his analyst. He felt that he had improved psychologically.

Mert's mother told her son how she had been aware of his fears. She slept in the same room with him that evening since she thought that he might be afraid to stay in a room alone after the funeral of his cousin that they had attended that day. The patient did not object to this. But he kept wondering what Dr. Ufuk would think of his visit to his childhood home after a death occurred while he was searching for information about the Armenians in Anatolia and his sleeping in the same room with his mother.

When he started to see Dr. Ufuk again he described what had happened when she was away and then added: "My hair is starting to turn grey. I am now forty-eight years old. I feel much better about myself." But referring to his allowing his mother to sleep in the same room with him he added: "I am still not completely free of my symptoms." Then he started talking about Mesut Yılmaz, a Turkish politician who was the head of the *Anavatan* (Motherland) political party, and who served as the minister of culture and tourism and three times as Turkish prime minister. Mert declared: "I know that Mesut Yılmaz comes from a family with *Hemşinli* origin. He was not a 'fake' Turk. I can also change and feel comfortable about myself."

CHAPTER ELEVEN

Behavioral Changes

Changes in Mert's life and his relationships with others had started prior to his "second look" experiences and his thinking of Mesut Yılmaz as a role model. While he was telling his secrets to Dr. Ufuk, he and his wife asked their son to sleep in another room, but Süleyman's sleeping in another room by himself comfortably would take some time. Mert's wife would not close the parental bedroom door in case Süleyman should wake up frightened or needing something. In fact, for some time the teenager would visit the parental bedroom during the night, and sometimes Mert's wife would go to her son's bedroom and sleep there. In short, the sexual relationship between Mert and his wife could not be resumed even though the boy no longer slept in the parental bedroom.

Mert took his son to see a psychologist. This psychologist asked Süleyman to draw a picture of his family members and close relatives. When Mert saw what his son drew he felt bad. His son had put him and his paternal grand-parents far away from him. Mert, recalling his distant relationship with his father, began wanting to find ways to develop a close father–son relation-ship with Süleyman. Soon Süleyman would begin seeing the psychologist once a week.

Mert was aware that he had been seeing Dr. Ufuk for a year. He told her that it was time for him to take some action in order to facilitate his "get-ting well as soon as possible." He confessed that recently he was involved in activities ranging from visiting an acupuncturist to swimming regularly at his sports club and to putting his feet in warm salty water, and so on. He referred to all these activities as "therapy." He had kept his new "therapies" a secret from Dr. Ufuk, and this reminded him of how, as a young man, he would secretly take drugs that were supposed to make his penis bigger. Dr. Ufuk, without using technical terms, told Mert how he had gone through second look experiences and how he had utilized his new insights about being a *Hemşinli* and having a difficult childhood to give up his phobia of cemeteries. She suggested that he did not need new independent "therapies" and be involved in them on his own. She added: "I am still here. Let us continue to work together." Mert responded: "I had a life alone. I had secrets. Now I want to live up to my emotions." He started crying and kept crying on the couch until the session ended. This was his first highly emotional session since the beginning of his analysis after he sang a song in his childhood language.

Dr. Ufuk noticed that Mert had bought a shirt that had the same fabric pattern as a dress she had often worn recently during her sessions with her patients. She thought that her analysand was making further efforts to identify with her and also to feel close to her. She did not verbalize her observation during her sessions with Mert. Before lying on the couch and before leaving his analyst's office, Mert would look at Dr. Ufuk's face adoringly. Then Mert openly developed an intense "erotic transference." He did not pick Dr. Ufuk as the target of his erotic feelings, however; his feelings were displaced on his wife. Since Mert was not talking about Dr. Ufuk while describing his sexual desires, the analyst did not wish to frighten him by referring to herself as being the patient's target of sexualized transference expectations. Dr. Ufuk did not interfere. We also considered the possibility of Mert's wife responding to him in a positive manner.

Mert recalled how his wife used to tell him, "You are not normal." He used to think that she meant, "You are a villager. You are an Armenian." Now he asked his wife if they could have a serious talk. When she sat down to listen to him, Mert was also able to tell her openly that he would feel very angry whenever he felt humiliated by her. He described certain cultural differences between them and expressed his determination to make attempts to socialize more. He added that he also wanted to resume sexual relations with her. He asked to keep their bedroom private. He suggested that they watch a pornographic film in order for both of them to be sexually stimulated. His wife refused to watch the film, but one evening Mert walked naked in the bedroom and his wife agreed to have sex with him. He had a premature ejaculation, but he knew that he would not give up and would continue his efforts to be a lover for his wife.

Meanwhile Mert reduced his visits to the widow to once a week. Then one day, instead of having sex with the widow, he also sat down with her, explaining how changes were taking place in him and how the time had come to stop his relationship with her. He sensed that the widow responded with empathy. Because he spent long hours with the widow on that day he came to his house late. His wife questioned him about why he was late. Her interest in him pleased Mert, but he also experienced fear. What would happen if his wife found out about the widow? He did not wish to go through a divorce. He realized that he was never in love with the widow.

The next week he visited the widow and again he did not make love to her. She shared her financial worries with Mert. He promised to give her money so that she would be able to pay her rent without difficulty for some years to come. His separation from the widow took place without much difficulty. When he went to his home, once more he talked with his wife about how he, a villager and *Hemşinli*, and she a city person, could become closer and be sexual partners. They made love and this time he did not have a premature ejaculation.

Mert bought a very expensive car for his wife. Then he realized that he had gone back to his old habit of "buying" her attention and love. He took her out for a walk and saw a man who was selling roses. This time, he wanted to be a socialized and sophisticated husband; he bought a rose for his wife. After paying the seller he waited to receive the change the man was supposed to give him instead of leaving what the seller owed back as a tip. This upset his wife. He was still a "fake" man. He told Dr. Ufuk that he would not give up and he would continue to improve his relationship with his wife. The analyst gave him no advice.

That evening he had a dream. In the dream he was in a cemetery. He was not afraid. He was busy putting a big gravestone on a plot of ground, but he knew that there was no dead person under the stone. He was not putting down a gravestone to keep a ghost from coming up. When he woke up he thought that he was burying his childhood difficulties. Soon after this dream he thought more about being a different father for his son. He made plans for the boy to participate in a school program in which a group of youngsters of his son's age would spend time away from their homes at a camp. When he told this to his wife she would not believe that her husband had made such an arrangement. She did not want Süleyman to sleep away from home. But Mert's plan did not change. The wife developed a coughing spell. Dr. Ufuk told Mert that it might take some time for his wife to adjust to changes in her husband.

Mert visited the widow once more to be sure that she was doing well. This visit, also without any sexual encounter, went well. He had another long talk with his wife and suggested they lock their bedroom at night time and not wear any clothing when they went to bed together. His wife told him how he was a changed man. She, naked, asked him to massage her back. Mert was overwhelmed by this; he perceived his wife as a woman who loved him. While reporting this on the couch, the first thing that came to Mert's mind was his leaving the village at age seventeen on a bus to go to Ankara and seeing his father waving at him. This was his main memory of his father loving him. Now his wife was loving him. He declared: "Analysis has opened my horizon. I have become a person who is wanted by people around me."

What Dr. Ufuk and I observed seemed to suggest an approval from an oedipal father for his son to find his own woman. But we knew that Mert basically was dealing with his pre-oedipal issues. He was identifying with the "analytic object" and evolving new ego functions. He had another long conversation with his wife and explained further his understanding of their difficulty relating to one another as if he were a psychoanalyst. He kept his "erotic transference" to test if he could be a wanted and loved child/person. Earlier he had had a similar experience with his mother when he had talked to her as if he were a psychoanalyst describing unconscious factors playing a role in personality characteristics. Mert's wish and efforts to "get well" were moving too fast. Then he began exhibiting somatic recollections of his childhood and experienced a therapeutic regression.

CHAPTER TWELVE

Therapeutic Regression, Somatic Recollections, and Disappearance of Phobias

It rained heavily in Istanbul. Mert noticed how a street he was driving on looked like a river. When he came home he learned that a section of his basement was flooded, so he went down to look at the flooded area, which was being cleaned up by a worker. His mind became filled with images of dead Armenians thrown into a river or into the Canyon of Hell. He thought about his sister who had never gone to school and who never left their village. He visualized her physical appearance. Apparently, she was now overweight, had spent her entire life surrounded by her family members, and never cared about what was happening in the world. On the couch Mert asked himself two questions: "In comparison to my sister, am I still a *Hemşinli* or am I a sophisticated city person? Who am I?" During his next sessions he began demonstrating a preoccupation with his body and his physical health. Was his heart beating correctly? Could he move his arms and legs freely? Was he overweight? He began taking many different vitamins. Dr. Ufuk and I sensed that he was experiencing a regression expressed with somatic preoccupation. We hoped that this regression would be a therapeutic one.

Mert visited several laboratories for blood tests and then went to a physician. His sugar level was a little high, but he had no diabetes. He now connected all his psychological fears to having a high sugar level. He asked, "Am I going through the menopause?" When Dr. Ufuk suggested that he let his mind wander about his having a "menopause," Mert recalled having a dream the previous evening. In the dream he was at a place like a harem, filled with women who, unlike men, would have a menopause. Mert recalled his babyhood and childhood and his being taken care of, not by a mother but by many "mothers." He began to report more data about his childhood. His mother had told him that when he was a baby she would leave him after feeding him in the morning and would not see him again until the evening. He was also told that he was taken care of by his paternal grandmother most of the time after his birth with some help from his aunts and his sister. Dr. Ufuk learned that he had been swaddled for a longer time than was customary, for over a year, until he started walking. From an aunt he had heard that he had been swaddled very heavily, his arms and legs tightly squeezed. He learned that he could not lie on his side, and always had to lie on his back. This aunt told him how one day he had fallen off a couch while swaddled and had stayed on the floor for a long time unable to move. On the couch Mert began to experience more and more what he called "bodily fear," a sense of inability to move, accompanied by blurred images that he could not describe.

Removing the analyst from the analysand's sight and asking the analysand to lie on the couch invites the analysand into a therapeutic regression as the analysis progresses. Therapeutic regression is in the service of the analysand's increased ability to sense, authenticate, and explore his or her original childhood. This leads to the analysand's making pathological personality characteristics and symptoms "ego-alien." Experiencing this type of regression increases the analysand's ability to recognize his or her internal world and develop new relationships to the external environment. Earlier I (Volkan, 2010) wrote that the idea of regression giving way to a new psychic organization has been demonstrated in an individual's psychic developmental process and under certain clinical conditions. For example, in normal development, the natural regression that takes place during adolescence ushers in a new psychic organization (Blos, 1979); in uncomplicated mourning, after the loss of a love object, mourners experience regression before being able to reestablish an inner adaptation to their external reality that no longer contains the lost object (Pollock, 1989; Volkan, 1981; Volkan & Zintl, 1993). Young psychoanalysts should be careful not to interfere with their analysands' therapeutic regression with the anxiety-driven idea that the patient will disintegrate. In my opinion, without therapeutic regression the technique cannot be considered truly psychoanalytic. Premature oedipal interpretations—indeed, even any direct and insistent attention to such issues—preclude the development of therapeutic regression (Boyer, 1983; Ornstein & Ornstein, 1975; Rosenfeld, 1966; Volkan, 1976, 1993). Making "interpretations" will interfere with the analysand's therapeutic regression experience, which will be the basis for future therapeutic progress. However, the analyst can tell the analysand, without using technical terms, what the analysand is experiencing. This helps the therapeutic alliance; the analysand does not feel alone while going through a tough time; there is someone who understands.

Dr. Ufuk told Mert that as a baby and small child he did not have a language to name his experiences and his emotions. She added that he was revisiting such experiences on the couch. However, now he and his analyst could put names to his emotions. She asked him to name his bodily experience and blurred visual images and emotion. Mert's name for his experiences was "being smothered." He named his feeling as "rejection." He knew that later in his life he connected such an emotion with stories about Christian or Muslim Armenians.

During the sessions that followed Mert continued to put bodily feelings into words. He said that his body felt like a truck with tires empty of air. Dr. Ufuk sensed that Mert was talking about a heavily swaddled baby who could not move. Mert had started to run daily with Süleyman. Besides wanting to spend more time with his son, he wanted to be sure that he could move his body; it was not swaddled.

One day he was very surprised when his wife came to the bathroom while he was taking a bath and started rubbing his back with a washcloth. When he had talked to his wife about the *Hemşinli* culture he had mentioned how his mother used to rub his back with a sponge until he was twelve years old. By rubbing his back now, Mert felt that his wife was allowing herself to try a custom from his village. This time she talked with him and told him not to take so many vitamins and not to have so many bodily fears. He took his wife to his sports club and watched her swim. Unlike Mert, she was swimming slowly and she looked beautiful. He imagined that he could slow down too.

The widow was calling Mert about every other week. He spoke to her with kind words and reassurances of financial help. He did not seem to be very disturbed by this. He was handling the situation comfortably and realistically. Meanwhile his mother had started calling and asking him when he and his wife would have a second child. Mert spoke to his wife about the idea of a second child, and she was very open to it. She kissed him and said, "I love you." He responded, "I love you too." His association of this closeness with his wife was a memory of how people always ate dark bread in the village. "I was fourteen years old when I ate white bread for the first time; it tasted like I was having a fine pastry," he said. Now, he was feeling that he could have a city woman as a wife and lover, and this would be natural and acceptable.

A few days later it was the couple's fourteenth wedding anniversary. He bought flowers for his wife and took her to a fancy restaurant. On the way back home they sang together in the car. At home they made love. His wife said: "I've waited fourteen years for this." That night Mert had a dream, which he told Dr. Ufuk the next day. In the dream he was driving a truck and singing. He said: "I knew that the truck's tires were okay. My truck's tires are no longer empty." He added: "I feel like I am reborn. Also, do you know, my fears of dead people, ghosts, and graves have disappeared." He also stopped making somatic complaints.

CHAPTER THIRTEEN

Growing Up in a Different Way

During his somatic preoccupation and therapeutic regression Mert lost more than 40 kilos. His analyst was very much aware of this. She and I connected his weight loss with his therapeutic regression, his symbolically being a baby again. After stating "as if I am reborn," Mert wanted to see if there was a new way of growing up. He said: "I want a new childhood. I want a new honeymoon." Once more he started looking at his developmental history, his adolescence, and behavior patterns of his adult-hood in order to leave some experiences behind and find new ones. Dr. Ufuk heard new information about Mert's life. This would not change our under-standing of Mert's internal world; it would simply support what we already had gathered about his difficult childhood and adolescence passage.

Mert told his analyst that he was born during the spring season. On the farm there were no fruit trees, no flowers. Soon after his birth his father had to go away from the farm for his obligatory military service, and the mother was left with her daughter and a baby. The maternal grandmother had become a primary caregiver of the children. Mert once more described how they ate dark bread and feared going hungry.

After returning from military service, Mert's father had to work extremely hard on the farm. Mert said to Dr. Ufuk: "Do you know that my father did not know how to drive a car until he was seventy years old?" When the time arrived for collecting tea leaves, it had to be done within a week.

Mert recalled how as a youngster he also participated in the harvest. Once his fingers were infected and they hurt terribly. He also remembered how at age eleven he had to carry 40–50 kilograms of tea leaf in a bag on his back after one of his fingers was badly cut. He stated that when he was in Ankara there were days he was afraid of remaining hungry. "And, look at me now," he added. "I have more than 150 people working in my factory. I have business partners. Earning so much money did not change me. I told you earlier, in my dreams most of the time I see myself in my village. But things are changing now." Once more he spoke of feeling like a newborn baby. "I want to find out if there are new ways of growing up." He wanted a new type of life; he wanted to grow up very fast and without anxiety. Dr. Ufuk made sure that she was hearing where Mert was in his analytic journey. She told him that there was no need to be in a hurry. They would continue to examine together Mert's attempts to find a more comfortable life and recognize psychological obstructions so he could resolve them. Mert responded: "I am forty-eight years old. I am still alive. Yes, I can change without anxiety."

In the sessions that followed Mert turned his attention toward having a new baby. His analyst and I thought that his desire to have a new child was also connected with his wish to move out of his therapeutic regression and be born again. Dr. Ufuk chose not tell this to Mert so as not to hinder his progressive therapeutic efforts. Mert took Süleyman for a walk and told his son how he and his mother were planning to have a new baby. He was very pleased that this news made Süleyman happy. His son wanted to have a sibling. Then, a thought came to Mert's mind: He might stop having sex with his wife when she became pregnant because entering his wife might hurt the baby. He shared this thought with Dr. Ufuk and understood that the idea of refraining from sex was related to the old Mert when as a *Hemşinli* he could not be the lover of a city woman. This understanding also led to a behavioral change in Mert. During his marriage, after talking with his mother on the phone he would end up informing his wife about what his mother had said; but his wife would not want to listen. He now knew that in the past his urge to share his mother's thoughts, wishes, and desires with his wife was a symbolic effort in his mind to bring together his *Hemşinli* part with the imagined sophisticated city man part, but more importantly, to remember that he was both a *Hemşinli* and a city man. From then on, Mert stopped telling his wife about his phone conversations with his mother.

One of his workers who originated from the area where people of Hemshin descent live came to see him. This man was preparing to marry, but had recently learned that his fiancé was afraid of ghosts. He came to see his boss for advice. Should he take his future wife to see a *hodja*? Should she get an amulet? This interaction reminded Mert of his childhood. Reporting this to his analyst, he once more realized how his own fears of cemeteries and ghosts had disappeared. He smiled. The night after talking with this man Mert had a dream. In this dream he saw himself naked in water facing a fish, which did not scare him. He got out of the water soaking wet. Dr. Ufuk told him that his dream also illustrated his wish to be reborn again, be out of his mother's belly. Dr. Ufuk would not talk about the possible oedipal aspect of the dream; the idea of the fish representing his father's penis. Mert was not dealing with oedipal issues at this phase of his analysis. After this session Mert colored his hair in order cover the areas that were turning white. In fact, he looked younger. Dr. Ufuk made no comment about the idea of his coloring his hair also being connected with Mert's wish "to be born again." She wanted Mert to continue to change.

Mert has been in analysis for a year and three months. Dr. Ufuk and I were pleased about how his analysis was progressing. The widow, feeling satisfied with the financial support she had received from Mert, was no longer calling him. His sessions were mostly centering on his expectation of his wife's new pregnancy, his feeling more comfortable as a husband and as a businessman, and his spending more time with his son.

CHAPTER FOURTEEN

Conducting Analysis during Political Turmoil

Soon the political situation in Turkey would create a societal mess for many citizens. A little over a year before Mert started seeing Dr. Ufuk, on 28 May 2013, a wave of demonstrations and civil unrest had taken place in Istanbul following an urban development plan for Istanbul's Gezi Park at the center of the city, next to Taksim Square. Demonstrators were evicted from a sit-in at the park. I know that among these demonstrators there were some psychoanalysts. An estimated 5,000 demonstrations across Turkey followed, in which eleven people were killed and more than 8,000 injured. All these activities were connected to the Gezi Park event, which expressed many Turks' fears about governmental encroachment on the nation's secularism, freedom of the press, and related political issues. Although political divisions in Turkey were visible and on everyone's mind, during his analysis Mert did not talk about the Gezi Park events and the political climate. Now, as he was attempting a psychological rebirth, once more political issues started to dominate citizens' minds. A general election in June 2015 resulted in a hung parliament, and a second general election was scheduled for 1 November 2015.

During this time Mert's father-in-law started to exhibit extreme nationalistic sentiments. For the first time Dr. Ufuk heard that his wife's paternal great-grandfather had been an active leader of a group of people responsible for killing Christian Armenians in an eastern part of Anatolia in 1915.

In order to protect the identity of individuals in this book, I will not name this man. Mert wondered if this man was acting on his own in murdering and hurting Armenians or if he was following some kind of orders from the Ottoman government. He could not get a response about this from his father-in-law who still believed that the Hemshin people were originally from Scotland. When his father-in-law said, "We cut off Armenians' heads," this time Mert sensed his rage and wondered what kind of creature his father-in-law was. One of his daughters was married to a person of Hemshin descent and his other daughter's husband was Kurdish. Mert also heard from his wife that her mother's side of the family was of Greek descent and his father's side was of *Çerkez* origin; they were Circassian people who had come to Anatolia following the Russian conquest of the Caucasus in the nineteenth century, specifically after the Russian–Circassian war in 1864. They also talk about experiencing genocide that year at the hand of the Russians. Today there are around 1.5 million Circassians in Turkey who, like the Hemshenis, have been Turkified. They are Sunni Muslims. In fact, one of them, Çerkez Ethem, a militia leader, is a well-known hero who fought against the Allied powers after they invaded Anatolia following World War 1 and also played a role in the Turkish War of Independence. Since I do not know the life stories of Mert's father-in-law or this older man of Çerkez origin, I cannot tell why they were angry with the Armenian people. My knowledge of human history informs me that ethnic conflicts that inflame the protection and maintenance of large-group identities can lead to forced migrations, rapes, killing of children, and dehumanization anywhere in the world. We see such events at the present time. Erecting walls to keep others away is happening throughout the world (Arıboğan, 2018), while we are waiting to see if a wall between the United States and Mexico will be built. In earlier times the Caucasus and eastern Anatolia were locations where many such terrible events took place and where the raising of physical and psychological "walls" separating different large groups was a preoccupation.

Mert sat down with his wife and talked to her about his anger at her father and disappointment in him. His wife said: "You are an educated person. You are not like *Hemşinli* persons from your village." This time, however, she noticed how her remarks were hurtful for her husband. They made up and even talked about how *Hemşinli* people also have their prejudices. Mert declared: "I am forgetting the ghosts from my past." Mert in a dream saw his wife's breasts getting bigger and both of them having fun at a luxurious place.

The second 2015 general election in Turkey took place on 1 November, and the existing authoritarian government tightened its grip on power. This was rather unexpected for many intellectuals and secular citizens in general. During his sessions Mert did not say for whom he had voted and did not talk about politics. He brought a dream that he was in his village, but the village had changed drastically and looked modern. His car was in an auto park, and while he was leaving the park he drove very close to a wall, hitting it on one side, scratching the car. Mert took his car in for repairs. He and Dr. Ufuk realized that there was more work for him to do to firm up the changes in him.

A month after the second elections Dr. Ufuk noted a different Mert. He was coming to his sessions dressed differently. He was wearing expensive clothes and appearing as a rich, sophisticated businessman. He brought another dream in which there were more drastic changes in his village. In the dream he drove a car through a forest on a road surrounded by thorny plants and trees, but the road was stable and he was able to drive through without any problem. He entered his village, and this time the village looked more modern; there were even bars. He saw his father in a bar and hugged him. The older man could not believe that his son was so friendly. He sat at a table with his father and his father's friends and all ordered the Turkish national drink, *rakı*, and began drinking together. After reporting his dream, Mert informed his analyst that he had started to call his mother every ten days or so. Dr. Ufuk learned that Mert for years had habitually called his mother every other day. Now, he informed his analyst, he had given up this habit. Also, the widow was now completely out of his life. Dr. Ufuk and I thought that Mert's dream and his less frequent contact with his mother might signal that he was starting to deal with oedipal passage issues.

He was expecting to hear that his wife was pregnant, but it turned out that she was not. Mert stated that they would continue to try to have a new baby. Süleyman was hoping to have a sister, and Mert was excited to see that his son, like himself, was waiting to welcome a pregnancy. For the first time he went to Süleyman's school to observe his participation in school activities. He was happy that his son's treatment, along with time they were spending together, was boosting the teenager's self-esteem. Mert also described how another of his phobias had disappeared. First, he dreamt about going to high places without fear. After this he went to a high place in Istanbul and walked around to be sure that this phobia was gone. He moved his office at his hotel from the first to the top floor.

CHAPTER FIFTEEN

An Unexpected Ending

Mert told Dr. Ufuk that he and two partners recently had made an offer on a business deal worth tens of millions of dollars. It involved building a huge park surrounded with high buildings. They were having meetings with high-level municipal officials to finalize this process. Dr. Ufuk wondered if this was the reason Mert was dressing differently. Perhaps he was coming to her office after attending such meetings or going to such meetings following his psychoanalytic hour. Mert was now telling his analyst that he, his partners, and their lawyers were absolutely sure that their offer would be accepted very soon. The offers that were made by other firms were not at a level to constitute any serious competition. Mert was free to show himself as a successful businessman. He told Dr. Ufuk how pleased he was when his wife invited his younger sister and her *Hemşinli* husband for dinner. His wife was also waiting to have a new pregnancy test.

On the couch Mert was no longer looking into his childhood and developmental years. During one session he talked extensively about his perception of Turkey's political situation. He gave a long history of how the ruling party had come to power and described growing corruption in the country. "I would rather be dead than vote for people who are ruining honesty in the political system," he said. For the first time Dr. Ufuk heard how Mert had voted. When Dr. Ufuk called me for supervision she told me how Mert looked her directly in the eye as he was leaving her office, in a way suggesting that she should notice how well he was dressed, how he was a respectable business person, and how as a grown-up he could share his political views with another grown-up.

Then Mert did not show up for four sessions. When he finally came to see Dr. Ufuk the first thing he told her was how the municipality had given the business project to someone with close connections to the political party ruling the country. He was sure that an order to turn down his and his partners' offer had come from Ankara, from this political party's authorities. "I feel normal now. But my two partners are still devastated," he said. He did not sound "normal," and his disappointment was reflected in the way he talked. "You have to be on the side of the ruling political party now or your business can be ruined," he added. He described how much he and his partners had invested in the business project and how sure they had been of a positive outcome. When Dr. Ufuk called me for further supervision she ended up talking about her frustration over what was happening in Turkey socially, culturally, and especially politically. Religion was being used for political gain and she wondered if there would be pressure against practicing psychoanalysis. Some people on television were freely talking against Darwin and Freud and suggesting that their ideas should not be taught in Turkey since such ideas were incorrect; such ideas could not be accepted by Muslims. I listened to her with empathy.

Mert flew to another city for a short trip for another, smaller business deal. During his session following his return to Istanbul, he described what was happening to him. "While flying in the airplane I had no fear. My fear of high places is gone. My wife is now very nice to me. But some of the architects and engineers who had been working with me for a long time are leaving my firm. After we lost the big business project they felt that the future of my firm is not very good."

During his next psychoanalytic session he described how his firm was facing further unexpected difficulties. He sensed that the ruling political party was teaching him a lesson not to compete with anyone who was a party supporter. Apparently, some government inspectors were sent from Ankara to check on some of Mert and his partners' building projects in Istanbul. These inspectors were very open in demanding bribes from Dr. Ufuk's analysand, forcing him openly to support their political party and also to have his workers support the same party. "I am not Don Quixote," Mert murmured. Dr. Ufuk was moved when she noticed Mert's humiliation. She told him that she understood his difficulty and emotions facing such external political pressure and political corruption. Dr. Ufuk also felt very sad for her analysand, but she did not verbalize this feeling.

A week later Mert described how a person came to see him and told him where in Istanbul a relative of one of the highest-level politicians in the ruling political party lived. Mert was advised to go to see this person. This relative then would find a new partner who belonged to the ruling party to work with Mert. This was the only way Mert could retain his position in the business world. He told Dr. Ufuk how angry he had become and how he shouted "No!" to this person. When this session ended Dr. Ufuk noted that Mert had left money on her table, not only for one session but two sessions. Once more, since the beginning of his analysis, he was making her owe something to him. She planned to talk about this with Mert during their next session, but Mert did not show up. Instead, he sent a short email message to her which read, "Dear Dr. Ufuk, I cannot think of coming to psychoanalysis again. Thank you very much for all the help you have given me." Dr. Ufuk called me and asked if she should write back. I suggested that she should. She send Mert an email telling him that, in her mind, the most important thing for him would be to come to her office and talk about what was happening. Mert did not respond. Soon we realized that a most unexpected situation had occurred. Mert's analytic process would not continue.

Dr. Ufuk and I talked and tried to understand why Mert stopped coming to see her in spite of the fact that he was very aware of how lying on a psychoanalytic couch had given him necessary insights about his psychological problems and how he was making many positive changes. He had had a very workable therapeutic alliance with Dr. Ufuk. We wondered if the ruling political party's unbelievable interference with Mert's business and personal life had led Mert to return to being a "fake" Turk. However, there was no hint that the people connected with the ruling party were hurting and humiliating him because he was a *Hemşinli*. Their focus was on his not being a follower and supporter of their party. We also wondered if Mert realized that most likely he would soon face major financial difficulties and if this realization obliged him to do something to save his business and secure the future of his wife, his son, and the expected new baby. Did he go to the address he was given to accept a new partner linked to the ruling party? If he did something like this, we felt, he would be ashamed to come to see Dr. Ufuk and tell her what he had done. Obviously, these were only guesses.

Since Mert had left his analysis before being analyzed for a minimum of two years, Dr. Ufuk's institute would not accept her work with Mert as fulfilling the required work for her training. Some months later Dr. Ufuk started to analyze another individual as her second training case. She chose to continue to work with me, and I began supervising her for her new case. As months passed I kept thinking of Mert. Now and then I would ask Dr. Ufuk if he had gotten in touch with her, but he never did. I also noticed that Dr. Ufuk never tried to find out what had happened to Mert. Since I never knew Mert's last name, I could not look into it, even though I wanted to know what had happened to him. I decided not to ask Dr. Ufuk who Mert is. I kept my supervisor identity in check.

Last Comments

During the last decade I published books describing psychoanalytic processes from their beginning to their termination (Volkan, 2010, 2014b, 2015a, 2015b; Volkan with Fowler, 2009). During the age of "psychoanalytic pluralism" I thought that there is a need for psychoanalysts to present total case reports in order to illustrate how their different methods are applied to improve their analysands' psychological health. The reader may wonder why I chose an unfinished psychoanalytic process to present in this book. I chose this case because it illustrates very clearly that without knowing the analysand's history and background it would be impossible to fully understand his internal world. Most likely the existing political situation was the primary factor in his terminating analysis. Furthermore, this case induced specific memories, thoughts, and feelings in the psychoanalytic supervisor. I could not find references describing a supervisor's reactions to the individual being analyzed by the supervised analyst. I hope that my attempting to do this may open a door for others to explore this topic.

My decades-long unofficial work in international relations and in many different countries has taught me the reality that human beings everywhere are the same. But history, culture, and politics lead to different individualized and collective expressions of human perceptions, emotions, and thoughts. Some expressions, especially those connected to the maintenance and protection of our large-group identities, under certain conditions, including having a destructive political leader, can become deadly (Suistola & Volkan, 2017). Such events create ghosts that haunt subsequent generations. The subject of this book, starting in his childhood, lived with such ghosts. In cases like his, psychoanalysts are required to study and learn the historical, cultural, and political issues linked to the analysand's life and help the person define and name such ghosts and tame their pathological impacts.

References

Abend, S. (1986). Countertransference, empathy, and the analytic ideal: The impact of life stresses on analytic capability. *Psychoanalytic Quarterly, 55*: 563–575.

Adler, E., & Bachant, L. (1996). Free association and analytic neutrality: The basic structure of the psychoanalytic situation. *American Journal of Psychoanalysis, 44*: 1021–1046.

Agatsuma, S. (2014). Differentiating two kinds of neutrality. *International Forum of Psychoanalysis, 23*: 238–245.

Akhtar, S. (2014). *Immigration and Acculturation: Mourning, Adaptation, and the Next Generation*. New York: Rowman & Littlefield.

Alderdice, J. (2007). The individual, the group and the psychology of terrorism. *International Review of Psychiatry, 19*: 201–209.

Alderdice, J. (2010). Off the couch and round the conference table. In: A. Lemma & M. Patrick (Eds.), *Contemporary Psychoanalytic Applications* (pp. 15–32). New York: Routledge.

Alpert, J. L., & Goren, E. R. (Eds.) (2017). *Psychoanalysis, Trauma, and Community: History and Contemporary Reappraisals*. New York: Routledge.

Apprey, M. (1993). The African-American experience: Forced immigration and transgenerational trauma. *Mind and Human Interaction, 4*: 70–75.

Apprey, M. (1998). Reinventing the self in the face of received transgenerational hatred in the African American community. *Mind and Human Interaction, 9*: 30–37.

Arıboğan, D. U. (2018). *Duvar: Tarih Geri Dönüyor* [Wall: Going Back in History]. Istanbul: Inkilap.

Arlow, J. (1973). Motivations for peace. In: H. Z. Winnik, R. Moses, & M. Ostow (Eds.), *Psychological Basis of War* (pp. 193–204). Jerusalem: Jerusalem Academic Press.

Arlow, J. (1991). Derivative manifestations of perversions. In: G. I. Fogel & W. A. Myer (Eds.), *Perversions and Near-Perversions in Clinical Practice: New Psychoanalytic Perspectives* (pp. 59–74). New Haven, CT: Yale University Press.

Auestad, L., Bohleber, W., Leo, G., Varvin, S., Volkan, V., & West, L. (2017). *Fundamentalism and Psychoanalysis*. Milan, Italy: Frencis Zero Press.

Blackman, J. (2018). Personal communication.

Blass, R. (2003). On ethical issues at the foundation of the debate over the goals of psychoanalysis. *International Journal of Psychoanalysis, 84*: 929–944.

Bloom, P. (2010). *How Pleasure Works: The New Science of Why We Like What We Like*. New York: W. W. Norton.

Blos, P. (1962). *On Adolescence*. New York: Free Press.

Blos, P. (1967). The second individuation process of adolescence. *Psychoanalytic Study of the Child, 22*: 162–186.

Blos, P. (1979). *The Adolescence Passage: Developmental Issues*. New York: International Universities Press.

Blum, H. P. (1985). Superego formation, adolescent transformation and the adult neurosis. *Journal of the American Psychoanalytic Association, 4*: 887–909.

Bohleber, W. (2003). Collective phantasms, destructiveness, and terrorism. In: S.Varvin & V. D. Volkan (Eds.), *Violence or Dialogue: Psychoanalytic Insights on Terror and Terrorism* (pp. 111–130). London: International Psychoanalytical Association.

Böhm, T., & Kaplan, S. (2011). *Revenge: On the Dynamics of Frightening Urge and Its Taming*. London: Karnac.

Bornstein, M. (Ed.) (1983). Values and neutrality in psychoanalysis. *Psychoanalytic Inquiry, 3*: 547–717.

Bowlby, J. (1988). *A Secure Base: Parent-Child Attachment and Healthy Human Development*. New York: Basic Books.

Boyer, L. B. (1983). *The Regressed Patient*. New York: Jason Aronson.

Brazelton, T. B., & Greenspan, S. I. (2000). *The Irreducible Needs of Children: What Every Child Must Have to Grow, Learn and Flourish*. Cambridge, MA: Perseus.

Brenner, I. (2002). Foreword. In: V. D. Volkan, G. Ast, & W. F. Greer, *The Third Reich in the Unconscious* (pp. xi–xvii). New York: Brunner-Routledge.

Brenner, I. (2014). *Dark Matters: Exploring the Realm of Psychic Devastation*. London: Karnac.

Cameron, N. (1961). Introjection, reprojection, and hallucination in the interaction between schizophrenic patient and therapist. *International Journal of Psychoanalysis, 42*: 86–96.

Cheour, M., Martynova, O., Näätänen, R., Erkkola, R., Sillanpää, M., Kero, P., Raz, A., Kaipio, M. L., Hiltunen, J., Aaltonen, O., Savela, J., & Hämäläinen, H. (2002). Speech sounds learned by sleeping newborns. *Nature, 415*: 599–600.

Eckstaedt, A. (1989). *Nationalsozialismus in der "zweiten Generation": Psychoanalyse von Hörigkeitsverhältnissen* [National Socialism in the Second Generation: Psychoanalysis of Master–Slave Relationships]. Frankfurt: Suhrkamp.

Ekstein, R. N. (1966). *Children of Time and Space, of Action and Impulse: Clinical Studies on the Psychoanalytic Treatment of Severely Disturbed Children*. East Norwalk, CT: Appleton-Century Crofts.

Elliott, M., Bishop, K., & Stokes, P. (2004). Societal PTSD? Historic shock in Northern Ireland. *Psychotherapy and Politics International, 2*: 1–16.

Emde, R. (1991). Positive emotions for psychoanalytic theory: Surprises from infancy research and new directions. *Journal of the American Psychoanalytic Association* (Supplement), *39*: 5–44.

Erikson, E. H. (1950). *Childhood and Society*. New York: W. W. Norton.

Erikson, E. H. (1956). The problem of ego identity. *Journal of the American Psychoanalytic Association, 4*: 56–121.

Erikson, E. H. (1959). *Identity and the Life Cycle*. New York: International Universities Press.

Erlich, H. S. (2010). A beam of darkness—understanding the terrorist mind. In: H. Brunning & M. Perini, *Psychoanalytic Perspectives on a Turbulent World* (pp. 3–15). London: Karnac.

Faimberg, H. (2005). *The Telescoping of Generations: Listening to the Narcissistic Links Between Generations*. London: Routledge.

Falzeder, E., & Brabant, E. (2000). *The Correspondence of Sigmund Freud and Sándor Ferenczi, Vol. 3, 1920–1933*. P. T. Hoffer (Trans.). Cambridge, MA: Harvard University Press.

Fenichel, O. (1945). *The Psychoanalytic Theory of Neurosis*. New York: W. W. Norton.

Fonagy, P., & Target, M. (1996). Playing with reality: 1: Theory of mind and the normal development of psychic reality. *International Journal of Psychoanalysis, 77*: 217–234.

Fornari, F. (1966). *The Psychoanalysis of War*. A. Pfeifer (Trans.). Bloomington, IN: Indiana University Press, 1975.

Fraiberg, S., Adelson, E., & Shapiro, V. (1975). Ghosts in the nursery: A psychoanalytic approach to the problems of impaired infant–mother relationships. *Science Direct, Journal of the American Academy of Child Psychiatry, 14*(3): 387–421.

Freud, A. (1936). *The Writings of Anna Freud. Vol. 1–4*. New York: International Universities Press, 1968.

Freud, A. (1954). The widening scope of indications for psychoanalysis. In: *The Writings of Anna Freud, Vol. 4* (pp. 356–376). New York: International Universities Press, 1968.

Freud, S. (1896c). The aetiology of hysteria. *S. E.*, *3*: 187–221. London: Hogarth.

Freud, S. (1905d). *Three Essays on the Theory of Sexuality. S. E.*, *7*: 123–243. London: Hogarth.

Freud, S. (1910d). The future prospects of psycho-analytic psychotherapy. *S. E.*, *11*: 139–152. London: Hogarth.

Freud, S. (1915a). Observations on transference-love (further recommendations on the technique of psycho-analysis, III). *S. E.*, *12*: 157–172. London: Hogarth.

Freud, S. (1919a). Lines of advance in psycho-analytic therapy. *S. E.*, *17*: 157–168. London: Hogarth.

Freud, S. (1920g). *Beyond the Pleasure Principle. S. E.*, *18*: 7–64. London: Hogarth.

Freud, S. (1925d). *An Autobiographical Study. S. E.*, *20*: 7–70. London: Hogarth.

Freud, S. (1933a). Femininity. In *New Introductory Lectures on Psycho-Analysis. S. E.*, *22*: 112–135. London: Hogarth.

Freud, S. (1933b). *Why War? S. E.*, *22*: 197–215. London: Hogarth.

Freud, S. (1940a). *An Outline of Psycho-analysis. S. E.*, *23*: 211–253. London: Hogarth.

Fromm, G. (Ed.) (2011). *Lost in Transmission: Studies of Trauma Across Generations*. London: Karnac.

Frosch, J. (1954). Editor's note. *Journal of the American Psychoanalytic Association, 2*: 565–566.

Gill, M. (1994). *Psychoanalysis in Transition: A Personal View*. Hillsdale, NJ: Analytic Press.

Giovacchini, P. L. (1972). Interpretation and the definition of the analytic setting. In: P. L. Giovacchini (Ed.), *Tactics and Techniques in Psychoanalytic Therapy, Vol. II* (pp. 5–94). New York: Jason Aronson.

Glower, E. (1947). *War, Sadism, and Pacifism: Further Essays on Group Psychology and War*. London: Allen & Unwin.

Glower, E. (1955). *The Technique of Psychoanalysis*. New York: International Universities Press.

Greenson, R. (1958). Variations in classical psychoanalytic technique. *International Journal of Psychoanalysis, 39*: 200–201.

Greenspan, S. I. (1981). *Psychopathology and Adaptation in Infancy and Early Childhood*. New York: International Universities Press.

Grubrich-Simitis, I. (1979). Extremtraumatisierung als kumulatives Trauma. Psychoanalytische Studien über seelische Nachwirkungen der Konzentrationslagerhaft bei Überlebenden und ihren Kindern [Extreme traumatization as a cumulative trauma. Psychoanalytic studies on the mental effects of imprisonment in concentration camps on survivors and their children.] *Psyche, 33*: 991–1023.

Hamburger, A. (Ed.) (2018). *Trauma, Trust, and Memory: Social Trauma and Reconciliation in Psychoanalysis, Psychotherapy, and Cultural Memory.* New York: Routledge.

Hamburger, A., & Laub, D. (Eds.) (2017). *Psychoanalysis and Holocaust Testimony: Unwanted Memories of Social Trauma.* New York: Routledge.

Harris, A., Kalb, M., & Klebanoff, S. (Eds.) (2016a). *Demons in the Consulting Room: Echoes of Genocide, Slavery and Extreme Trauma in Psychoanalytic Practice.* New York: Routledge.

Harris, A., Kalb, M., & Klebanoff, S. (Eds.) (2016b). *Ghosts in the Consulting Room: Echoes of Trauma in Psychoanalysis.* New York: Routledge.

Haynal, A. E. (2005). In the shadow of controversy: Freud and Ferenczi 1925–33. *International Journal of Psychoanalysis, 86*: 457–466.

Hoffer, A. (1985). Towards a definition of neutrality. *Journal of the American Psychoanalytic Association, 31*: 771–795.

Hoffer, P. T. (2010). From elasticity to the confusion of tongues: A historical commentary on the technical dimension of the Freud/Ferenczi controversy. *Psychoanalytic Perspectives, 7*: 90–103.

Hollander, N. C. (1997). *Love in a Time of Hate: Liberation Psychology in Latin America.* New York: Other Press.

Hollander, N. C. (2009). When not knowing allies with destructiveness: Global warning and psychoanalytic ethical non-neutrality. *International Journal of Applied Psychoanalytic Studies, 6*: 1–11.

Hollander, N. C. (2010). *Uprooted Minds: Surviving the Political Terror in the Americas.* New York: Taylor & Francis.

Jacobson, E. (1954). Transference problems in the psychoanalytic treatment of severely depressive patients. *Journal of the American Psychoanalytic Association, 2*: 595–606.

Jokl, A. M. (1997). *Zwei Fälle zum Thema "Bewältigung der Vergangenheit"* [Two Cases Referring to the Theme of "Mastering the Past"]. Frankfurt: Jüdischer Verlag.

Kahn, C. (2008). *Undeterred, I Made It In America.* Bloomington, IN: AuthorHouse.

Kakar, S. (1996). *The Colors of Violence: Cultural Identities, Religion, and Conflict.* Chicago, IL: University of Chicago Press.

Kandel, E. R. (1998). A new intellectual framework for psychiatry. *American Journal of Psychiatry, 155*: 457–469.

Kernberg, O. F. (1975). *Borderline Conditions and Pathological Narcissism*. New York: Jason Aronson.

Kernberg, O. F. (1976). Technical considerations in the treatment of borderline personality organization. *Journal of the American Psychoanalytic Association, 30*: 795–829.

Kernberg, O. F. (1980). *Internal World and External Reality: Object Relations Theory Applied*. New York: Jason Aronson.

Kernberg, O. F. (1984). *Severe Personality Disorders: Psychotherapeutic Strategies*. New Haven, CT: Yale University Press.

Kernberg, O. F. (2003a). Sanctioned political violence: A psychoanalytic view—Part 1. *International Journal of Psychoanalysis, 84*: 683–698.

Kernberg, O. F. (2003b). Sanctioned political violence: A psychoanalytic view—Part 2. *International Journal of Psychoanalysis, 84*: 953–968.

Kestenberg, J. S. (1982). A psychological assessment based on analysis of a survivor's child. In: M. S. Bergman & M. E. Jucovy (Eds.), *Generations of the Holocaust* (pp. 158–177). New York: Columbia University Press.

Kestenberg, J. S., & Brenner, I. (1996). *The Last Witness*. Washington, DC: American Psychiatric Press.

Keval, N. (2016). *Racist States of Mind: Understanding of the Perversion of Curiosity and Concern*. London: Karnac.

Klautau, P., & Coelho, N. (2013). On psychic reality and neutrality: Empathy and the work of construction in countertransference. *International Forum of Psychoanalysis, 22*: 142–148.

Klein, M. (1946). Notes on some schizoid mechanisms. In: J. Riviere (Ed.), *Development of Psychoanalysis* (pp. 292–320). London: Hogarth.

Klein, M. (1961). *Narrative of a Child Analysis: The Conduct of the Psychoanalysis of Children as Seen in the Treatment of a Ten-Year-Old Boy*. London: Hogarth, 1975.

Kogan, I. (1995). *The Cry of Mute Children: A Psychoanalytic Perspective of the Second Generation of the Holocaust*. London: Free Association.

Kogan, I. (2004). The role of the analyst in the analytic cure during times of chronic crises. *Journal of the American Psychoanalytic Association, 52*: 735–757.

Kohut, H. (1971). *The Analysis of the Self: A Systematic Approach to the Psychoanalytic Treatment of Narcissistic Personality Disorders*. New York: International Universities Press.

Kramer, S., & Akhtar, S. (Eds.) (1991). *The Trauma of Transgression*. Northvale, NJ: Jason Aronson.

Kris, A. (1982). *Free Associations*. New Haven, CT: Yale University Press.

Krystal, H. (Ed.) (1968). *Massive Psychic Trauma*. New York: International Universities Press.

Kuriloff, E. A. (2013). *Contemporary Psychoanalysis and the Legacy of the Third Reich: History, Memory, Tradition*. New York: Routledge.

Laplanche, J., & Pontalis, J.-B. (1973). *The Language of Psycho-Analysis*. D. Nicholson-Smith (Trans.). New York: W. W. Norton.

Lappi, H., Valkonen-Korhonen, M., Georgiadis, S., Tarvainen, M. P., Tarkka, I. M., Karjalainen, P. A., & Lehtonen, J. (2007). Effects of nutritive and non-nutritive sucking on infant heart rate variability during the first 6 months of life. *Infant Behavior Development, 30*: 546–556.

Laub, D., & Auerhahn, N. C. (1993). Knowing and not knowing massive trauma: Forms of traumatic memory. *International Journal of Psychoanalysis, 74*: 287–302.

Laub, D., & Podell, D. (1997). Psychoanalytic listening to historical trauma: The conflict of knowing and the imperative act. *Mind and Human Interaction, 8*: 245–260.

Lehtonen, J. (2016). Self before self: On the scenic model of the early embodied self. *Journal of Consciousness Studies, 23*: 214–236.

Levine, H. (Ed.) (1990). *Adult Analysis and Childhood Sexual Abuse*. Hillside, NJ: Analytic Press.

Loewald, H. W. (1960). On the therapeutic action of psychoanalysis. *International Journal of Psychoanalysis, 41*: 16–33.

Loewenberg, P. (1991). Uses of anxiety. *Partisan Review, 3*: 514–525.

Loewenberg, P. (1995). *Fantasy and Reality in History*. London: Oxford University Press.

Mack, J. E. (1979). Foreword. In: V. D. Volkan, *Cyprus: War and Adaptation* (pp. ix–xxi). Charlottesville, VA: University of Virginia Press.

Mahler, M. S. (1968). *On Human Symbiosis and the Vicissitudes of Individuation*. New York: International Universities Press.

Mahler, M., Pine, F., & Bergman, A. (1975). *The Psychological Birth of the Infant: Symbiosis and Individuation*. New York: Basic Books.

McCarthy, J. (1995). *Death and Exile: The Ethnic Cleansing of Ottoman Muslims, 1981–1922*. Princeton, NJ: Darwin.

Mitscherlich, A. (1971). Psychoanalysis and aggression of large groups. *International Journal of Psychoanalysis, 52*: 161–167.

Mitscherlich, A., & Mitscherlich, M. (1973). *Die Unfähigkeit zu trauern: Grundlagen kollektiven Verhaltens* [The Inability to Mourn: Principals of Collective Behavior]. Munich: Piper.

Moore, B. E., & Fine, B. D. (Eds.) (1990). *Psychoanalytic Terms and Concepts.* New York: American Psychoanalytic Association.

Moses, R. (1982). The group-self and the Arab-Israeli conflict. *International Review of Psycho-Analysis, 9*: 55–65.

Mucci, C. (2013). *Beyond Individual and Collective Trauma: Intergenerational Transmission, Psychoanalytic Treatment, and the Dynamics of Forgiveness.* London: Karnac.

Muller-Paisner, V. (2005). *Broken Chain: Catholics Uncover the Holocaust's Hidden Legacy and Discover Their Jewish Roots.* Charlottesville, VA: Pitchstone.

Naso, R. C., & Mills, J. (Eds.) (2016). *Humanizing Evil: Psychoanalytic, Philosophical and Clinical Perspectives.* New York: Routledge.

Niederland, W. (1961). The problem of the survivor. *Journal of the Hillside Hospital, 10*: 233–247.

Niederland, W. (1968). Clinical observations on the "survivor syndrome". *International Journal of Psychoanalysis, 49*: 313–315.

Novey, S. (1968). *The Second Look: The Reconstruction of Personal History in Psychiatry and Psychoanalysis.* Baltimore, MD: Johns Hopkins University Press.

Ofer, G. (Ed.) (2017). *Bridge Over Troubled Waters: Conflicts and Reconciliation in Groups and Societies.* London: Karnac.

Olsson, P. (2007). *The Cult of Osama: Psychoanalyzing Bin Laden and His Magnetism for Muslim Youth.* New York: Praeger.

Olsson, P. (2014). *The Making of a Homegrown Terrorist: Brainwashing Rebels in Search of a Cause.* New York: Praeger.

Olsson, P. (in press). *Janusian Days: A Memoir of an Almost Old Psychiatrist.*

Opher-Cohn, L., Pfäfflin, J., Sonntag, J. B., Klose, B., & Pogany-Wnendt, P. (Eds.) (2000). *Das Ende der Sprachlosigkeit? Auswirkungen traumatischer Holocausterfahrungen über mehrere Generationen* [The End of Speechlessness? The Effects of Experiencing the Holocaust over Several Generations]. Giessen: Psychosozial Verlag.

Ornstein, A., & Goldman, S. (2004). *My Mother's Eyes: Holocaust Memories of a Young Girl.* Covington, KY: Clerisy.

Ornstein, A., & Ornstein, P. H. (1975). On the interpretive process in schizophrenia. *International Journal of Psychoanalytic Psychotherapy, 4*: 219–271.

Ornstein, P. H., & Epstein, H. (2015). *Looking Back: Memoirs of a Psychoanalyst.* Lexington, MA: Plunkett Lake.

Öztürk, O. M., & Volkan, V. D. (1971). The theory and practice of psychiatry in Turkey. *American Journal of Psychotherapy, 25*: 240–271.

Paláez, M. G. (2009). Trauma theory in Sándor Ferenczi's writings, 1931–1932. *International Journal of Psychoanalysis, 90*: 1217–1233.

Parens, H. (2004). *Renewal of Life: Healing from the Holocaust.* Rockville, MD: Schriber.

Perdigão, H. G. (2018). Challenges in transcultural analyses. Paper presented at the Annual Meeting of the American Psychoanalytic Association, New York, February 15.

Pollock, G. (1989). *The Mourning-Liberation Process*, 2 vols. Madison, CT: International Universities Press.

Purhonen, M., Kilpeläinen-Lees, R., Valkonen-Korhonen, M., Karhu, J., & Lehtonen, J. (2005). Four-month-old infants process own mother`s voice faster than unfamiliar voices—electrical signs of sensitization in infant brain. *Cognitive Brain Research, 3*: 627–633.

Rachman, A. W. (1997). The suppression and censorship of Ferenczi's "Confusion of Tongues" paper. *Psychoanalytic Inquiry, 17*: 459–485.

Rangell, L. (2003). Affects: In an individual and a nation. First Annual Volkan Lecture, November 15, University of Virginia, Charlottesville, VA.

Rapaport, D. (1951). *Organization and Pathology of Thought: Selected Papers.* New York: Columbia University Press.

Roazen, P. (1974). *Freud and His Followers.* New York: Alfred A. Knopf.

Róheim, G. (1943). The origin and function of culture. *Nervous and Mental Diseases Monograph #69.* New York.

Rosenfeld, H. A. (1966). Discussion of "Office treatment of schizophrenic patients" by L. B. Boyer. *Psychoanalytic Forum, 1*: 351–353.

Rothstein, A. (Ed.) (1984). *The Reconstruction of Trauma: Its Significance in Clinical Work.* Madison, CT: International Universities Press.

Sachs, D. (2011). A history of new groups. In: P. Loewenberg & N. L Thomson (Eds.), *100 Years of the IPA: The Centenary History of the International Psychoanalytical Association—1910–2010* (pp. 448–454). London: Karnac.

Samberg, E. (2004). Resistance: How do we think of it in the twenty-first century? *Journal of the American Psychoanalytic Association, 52*: 243–253.

Scharff, D. E. (2018). Analytic forays in China. *The American Psychoanalyst, 52*: 11–13.

Scharff, D. E., & Scharff, J. S. (2011). *The Interpersonal Unconscious.* New York: Jason Aronson.

Schützenberger, A. A. (1998). *The Ancestor Syndrome: Transgenerational Psychotherapy and the Hidden Links in the Family Tree.* New York: Routledge.

Searles, H. F. (1979). *Countertransference and Related Subjects*. New York: International Universities Press.

Šebek, M. (1992). Anality in the totalitarian system and the psychology of post-totalitarian society. *Mind and Human Interaction, 4*: 52–59.

Šebek, M. (1994). Psychopathology of everyday life in the post-totalitarian society. *Mind and Human Interaction, 5*: 104–109.

Seligman, S. (2018). *Relationships in Development: Infancy, Intersubjectivity, and Attachment*. New York: Routledge.

Shapiro, E., & Carr, A. W. (1993). *Lost in Familiar Places: Creating New Connections between the Individual and Society*. New Haven, CT: Yale University Press.

Shapiro, T. (1984). On neutrality. *Journal of the American Psychoanalytic Association, 32*: 269–282.

Sharpe, E. (1950). *Collected Papers on Psycho-Analysis*. London: Hogarth.

Shengold, L. (1989). *Soul Murder*. New Haven, CT: Yale University Press.

Spitz, R. (1965). *The First Year of Life*. New York: International Universities Press.

Stern, D. N. (1985). *The Interpersonal World of the Infant: A View from Psychoanalysis and Developmental Psychology*. New York: Basic Books.

Stone, L. (1954). The widening scope of indications for psychoanalysis. *Journal of the American Psychoanalytic Association, 2*: 567–594.

Stone, L. (1961). *The Psychoanalytic Situation*. New York: International Universities Press.

Streeck-Fischer, A. (1999). Naziskins in Germany: How traumatization deals with the past. *Mind and Human Interaction, 10*: 84–97.

Strozier, C., Terman, D., & Jones, J. (Eds.) (2010). *The Fundamentalist Mindset: Psychological Perspectives on Religion, Violence, and History*. Oxford: Oxford University Press.

Suistola, J., & Volkan, V. D. (2017). *Religious Knives: Historical and Psychological Dimensions of International Terrorism*. Durham, N C: Pitchstone.

Tähkä, V. (1993). *Mind and Its Treatment: A Psychoanalytic Approach*. Madison, CT: International Universities Press.

Varvin, S., & Volkan, V. D. (Eds.) (2003). *Violence or Dialogue: Psychoanalytic Insights on Terror and Terrorism*. London: International Psychoanalytical Association.

Volkan, V. D. (1976). *Primitive Internalized Object Relations: A Clinical Study of Schizophrenic, Borderline, and Narcissistic Patients*. New York: International Universities Press.

Volkan, V. D. (1979). *Cyprus—War and Adaptation: A Psychoanalytic History of Two Ethnic Groups in Conflict*. Charlottesville, VA: University of Virginia Press.

Volkan, V. D. (1981). *Linking Objects and Linking Phenomena: A Study of the Forms, Symptoms, Metapsychology and Therapy of Complicated Mourning*. New York: International Universities Press.

Volkan, V. D. (1988). *The Need to Have Enemies and Allies: From Clinical Practice to International Relationships*. Northvale, NJ: Jason Aronson.

Volkan, V. D. (1993). Countertransference reactions commonly present in the treatment of patients with borderline personality organization. In: A. Alexandris & C. Vaslamatis (Eds.), *Countertransference and How It Affects the Interpretive Work* (pp. 147–163). London: Karnac.

Volkan, V. D. (1997). *Bloodlines: From Ethnic Pride to Ethnic Terrorism*. New York: Farrar, Straus and Giroux.

Volkan, V. D. (2004). *Blind Trust: Large Groups and Their Leaders in Times of Crises and Terror*. Charlottesville, VA: Pitchstone.

Volkan, V. D. (2006). *Killing in the Name of Identity: A Study of Bloody Conflicts*. Charlottesville, VA: Pitchstone.

Volkan, V. D. (2009). The next chapter: Consequences of societal trauma. In: P. Gobodo-Madikizela & C. van der Merve (Eds.), *Memory, Narrative and Forgiveness: Perspectives of the Unfinished Journeys of the Past* (pp. 1–26). Cambridge: Cambridge Scholars Publishing.

Volkan, V. D. (2010). *Psychoanalytic Technique Expanded: A Textbook of Psychoanalytic Treatment*. Istanbul: oa Publishing.

Volkan, V. D. (2011). Psychoanalysis, Turkey, and the IPA. In: P. Loewenberg & N. L Thomson (Eds.), *100 Years of the IPA: The Centenary History of the International Psychoanalytical Association—1910–2010* (pp. 419–434). London: Karnac.

Volkan, V. D. (2013). *Enemies on the Couch: A Psychopolitical Journey through War and Peace*. Durham, NC: Pitchstone.

Volkan, V. D. (2014a). *Psychoanalysis, International Relations, and Diplomacy: A Sourcebook on Large-Group Psychology*. London: Karnac.

Volkan, V. D. (2014b). *Animal Killer: Transmission of War Trauma from One Generation to the Next*. London: Karnac.

Volkan, V. D. (2015a). *A Nazi Legacy: A Study of Depositing, Transgenerational Transmission, Dissociation and Remembering through Action*. London: Karnac.

Volkan, V. D. (2015b). *Would-Be Wife Killer: A Clinical Study of Primitive Mental Functions, Actualized Unconscious Fantasies, Satellite States, and Developmental Steps*. London: Karnac.

Volkan, V. D. (2017). *Immigrants and Refugees: Trauma, Perennial Mourning, and Border Psychology*. London: Karnac.

Volkan, V., & Ast, G. (1994). *Spektrum des Narziβmus.* Göttingen, Germany: Vandenhoeck & Ruprecht.

Volkan, V. D., Ast, G., & Greer, W. F. (2002). *The Third Reich in the Unconscious: Transgenerational Transmission and Its Consequences.* New York: Brunner-Routledge.

Volkan, V. D., with Fowler, J. C. (2009). *Searching for a Perfect Woman: The Story of a Complete Psychoanalysis.* New York: Jason Aronson.

Volkan, V. D., & Itzkowitz, N. (1984). *The Immortal Atatürk: A Psychobiography.* Chicago, IL: University of Chicago Press.

Volkan, V. D., & Itzkowitz, N. (1994). *Turks and Greeks: Neighbours in Conflict.* Huntington, England: Eothen Press.

Volkan, V. D., & Kayatekin, S. (2006). Extreme religious fundamentalism and violence: Some psychoanalytic and psychopolitical thoughts. *Psyche & Geloof, 17*: 71–91.

Volkan, V. D., Makhashvili, N., Sariveladze, N., Vahip, I., & Gazzaeva, M. (2002). Final Report: IREX Black and Caspian Sea Collaborative Research Program—Gender Issues and Family Violence: Public Awareness and Services to Victims.

Volkan, V. D., & Zintl, E. (1993). *Life After Loss: Lessons of Grief.* New York: Charles Scribner's Sons.

Wallwork, E. (2005). Ethics in psychoanalysis. In: E. S. Person, A. M. Cooper, and G.O. Gabbard (Eds.), *The Textbook of Psychoanalysis* (pp. 281–297). Washington, DC: American Psychiatric Publishing.

Weigert, E. (1954). The importance of flexibility in psychoanalytic technique. *Journal of the American Psychoanalytic Association, 2*: 702–710.

Weston, M. C. (1997). When words lose their meaning: From societal crisis to ethnic cleansing. *Mind and Human Interaction, 8*: 20–32.

Wilson, C. (1981). *The Quest for Wilhelm Reich.* New York: HarperCollins.

Winnicott, D. W. (1953). Transitional objects and transitional phenomena: A study of the first not-me possession. *International Journal of Psycho-Analysis, 34*: 89–97.

Winnicott, D. W. (1965). *The Maturational Processes and the Facilitating Environment.* London: Hogarth.

Wolman, B. B. (Ed.) (1971). *The Psychoanalytic Interpretation of History.* New York: Basic Books.

Index